Introduction

The Science Coordination Group has been set up with the aim of producing
specialised revision material for National Curriculum Science.
This is one of a set of six books which provide concise coverage of the
National Curriculum Key Stage 4 syllabus for *GCSE Double Science*.
They are ideally suited to all syllabuses produced by the main Examination
Boards for GCSE Double Science, both Coordinated and Modular.

Throughout these books there is constant emphasis on the inescapable
need to ***keep learning the basic facts***. This simple message is hammered
home without compromise and without remorse, and whilst this traditionally
brutal philosophy may not be quite in line with some other approaches to
education, we still rather like it.   But only because it works.

Contents

Page References for Modular Syllabuses

Published by Coordination Group Publications
Typesetting and layout by The Science Coordination Group
Illustrations by: Sandy Gardner,   e-mail: zimkit@aol.com

Consultant Editor: Paddy Gannon BSc MA

Printed by Hindson Print, Newcastle upon Tyne.
Thanks to CorelDRAW for providing one or two jolly bits of clipart.

Current, Voltage and Resistance

Isn't electricity _great_. Mind you it's _pretty bad news_ if the words don't mean anything to you...

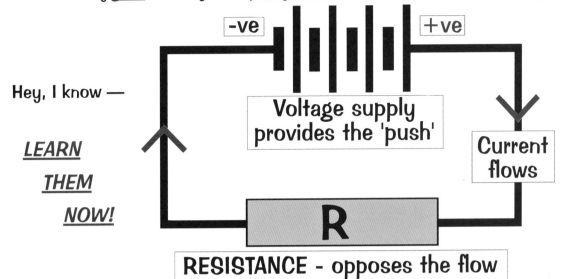

Hey, I know —

LEARN

THEM

NOW!

1) **CURRENT**   is the _flow of electrons_ round the circuit.

2) **VOLTAGE**   is the _driving force_ that pushes the current round. It's kind of like "_electrical pressure_".

3) **RESISTANCE**   is anything in the circuit which _slows the flow down_.

4) **THERE'S A BALANCE:**   The _voltage_ is trying to _push_ the current round the circuit, and the _resistance_ is _opposing_ it — the _relative sizes_ of the voltage and resistance decide _how big_ the current will be:

> If you _increase the VOLTAGE_ — then **MORE CURRENT** will flow.
> If you _increase the RESISTANCE_ — then **LESS CURRENT** will flow.

It's Just Like the Flow of Water Around a Set of Pipes

1) The _current_ is simply like the _flow of water_.
2) The _voltage_ is like the _pressure_ provided by a _pump_ which pushes the stuff round.
3) _Resistance_ is any sort of _constriction_ in the flow, which is what the pressure has to _work against_.
4) If you _turn up the pump_ and provide more _pressure_ (or "_voltage_"), the flow will _increase_.
5) If you put in more _constrictions_ ("_resistance_"), the flow (current) will _decrease_.

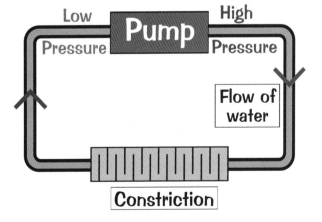

Understanding currents — easy as pie...

This page is all about electric current — what it is, what makes it move, and what tries to stop it. This is the most basic stuff on electricity there is. I assume you realise that you'll never be able to learn anything else about electricity until you know this stuff — don't you? Good-O.

Electric Charges and Current

Electric currents are purely and simply *the flow of ELECTRICAL CHARGES*. Know these details:

In Metals the Current is Carried by Electrons

1) Electric current will only flow if there are *charges* which can *move freely*.
2) Metals contain a *"sea" of free electrons* (which are negatively charged) and which *flow throughout the metal*.
3) This is what allows *electric current* to flow so well *in all metals*.

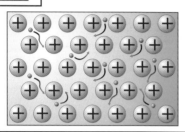

But Electrons Flow the Opposite Way to Conventional Current

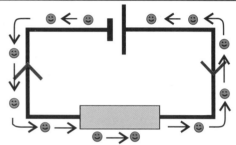

We *normally* say that current in a circuit flows from *positive to negative*. Alas electrons were discovered long after that was decided and they turned out to be *negatively charged* — *unlucky*. This means they *actually flow* from −ve to +ve, *opposite* to the flow of "*conventional current*".

In Electrolytes, Current is Carried by Both +ve and −ve Charges

1) *Electrolytes* are *liquids* which contain charges which can *move freely*.
2) They are either *ions dissolved in water*, like salt solution, or *molten ionic liquids*, like molten sodium chloride.
3) When a voltage is applied the *positive* charges move towards the *−ve*, and the *negative* charges move towards the *+ve*. This is an *electric current*.

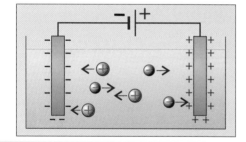

Direct Current — DC

In *DIRECT CURRENT*, the current *keeps flowing* in the *same direction* all the time.
Normal current from a *battery* is *direct current, DC*. The *CRO trace* is a *horizontal line*, as shown. *DC* is needed for *electronic circuits*, e.g. in TVs, computers, calculators, CD players etc.

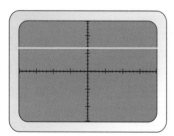

Alternating Current — AC

In *AC*, the current keeps *reversing its direction* back and forth. *Dynamos* and *power stations* produce *alternating current, AC*. *Mains electricity is AC* with a frequency of *50Hz*. That means it reverses direction *50 times every second*. The *CRO trace* is *always a wave*. *AC* is needed for *transformers* to work. (See P. 22) Electric motors can work off either AC or DC.

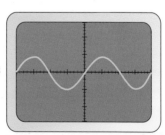

Electricity is like life — charges everywhere...

There's quite a few bits and bobs on this page, really. This is actually stuff that a lot of people tend to forget about. The thing is though, they mention all of this specifically in the syllabus and that means they're very likely to ask it in the Exams. So *learn it all*. Just *more easy marks*.

SECTION ONE — ELECTRICITY AND MAGNETISM

Energy in Circuits

You can look at _electrical circuits_ in _two ways_. The first is in terms of _a voltage pushing the current round_ and the resistances opposing the flow, as on P. 1. The _other way_ of looking at circuits is in terms of _energy transfer_. Learn _both_ and be ready to tackle questions about _either_.

Energy is Transferred from Cells and Other Sources

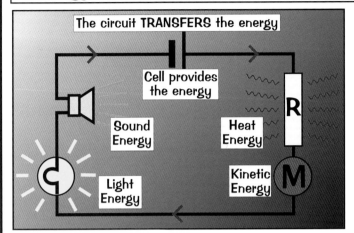

The circuit TRANSFERS the energy
Cell provides the energy
Sound Energy
Heat Energy
Light Energy
Kinetic Energy
R
M
C

1) Anything which _supplies electricity_ is also supplying _energy_.
   There are _four sources_ you need to _LEARN_:
   1) _CELLS_
   2) _BATTERIES_
   3) _GENERATORS_
   4) _SOLAR CELLS_
2) The energy is _transferred_ by the _electric circuit_ to _components_ such as lamps, resistors, bells, motors, LEDs, buzzers, etc.

3) These components perform their own _energy transfer_ and _convert_ the _electrical energy_ in the circuit into _other_ forms of energy: _HEAT_, _LIGHT_, _SOUND_ or _MOVEMENT_.
4) Don't forget that a _complete circuit_ is needed for the current to flow. If the circuit is _broken_ there will be _no current flow_ and _no transfer of energy_.

Electricity Can produce Four Effects:

Learn these _four examples_:

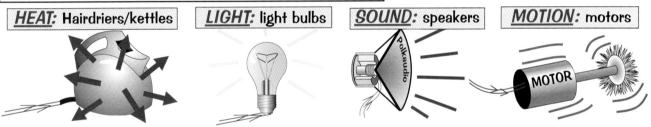

HEAT: Hairdriers/kettles   _LIGHT:_ light bulbs   _SOUND:_ speakers   _MOTION:_ motors

All Resistors produce Heat when a Current flows through them

1) This is important. Whenever a _current_ flows through anything with _electrical resistance_ (which is pretty well _everything_) then _electrical energy_ is converted into _heat energy_.
2) The _more current_ that flows, the _more heat_ is produced.
3) Also, a _bigger voltage_ means _more heating_, because it pushes _more current_ through.
4) However, the _higher_ you make the _resistance_, the _less heat_ is produced. This is because a higher resistance means _less current_ will flow, and that _reduces_ the heating.
5) The _amount of heat_ produced can be _measured_ by putting a resistor in a known amount of water or inside a solid block and measuring the _increase in temperature_.

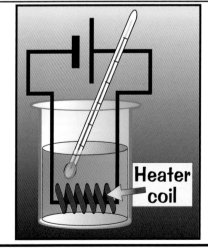

Heater coil

Electricity — it always creates a bit of a buzz...

I try to make it interesting, really I do. I mean, underneath it all, electricity is pretty good stuff, but somehow every page just seems to end up stuffed full of facts. Mind you there are some pretty pictures to jolly it up a bit — but in the end you've just gotta _learn it all_, and that's that.

The Standard Test Circuit

This is without doubt the most totally dog-standard circuit the world has ever known. So know it.

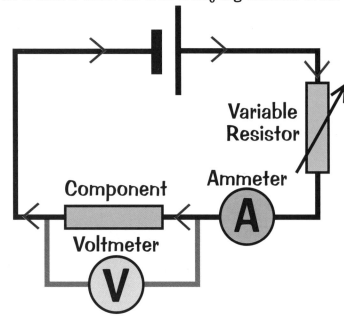

The Ammeter
1) Measures the _current_ (in _Amps_) flowing through the component.
2) Must be placed _in series_.
3) Can be put _anywhere_ in series in the _main circuit_, but _never in parallel_ like the voltmeter.

The Voltmeter
1) Measures the _voltage_ (in _Volts_) across the component.
2) Must be placed _in parallel_ around the _component under test_ — _NOT_ around the variable resistor or the battery!
3) The _proper_ name for "_voltage_" is "_potential difference_" or "_Pd_".

Five Important Points
1) This _very basic circuit_ is used for _testing components_, and for getting _V-I graphs_ for them.
2) The _component_, the _ammeter_ and the _variable resistor_ are all _in series_, which means they can be put _in any order_ in the main circuit. The _voltmeter_, on the other hand, can only be placed _in parallel_ around the _component under test_, as shown. Anywhere else is a definite _no-no_.
3) As you _vary_ the _variable resistor_ it alters the _current_ flowing through the circuit.
4) This allows you to take several _PAIRS OF READINGS_ from the _ammeter_ and _voltmeter_.
5) You can then _plot_ these values for _current_ and _voltage_ on a _V-I graph_, like the ones below.

Four Hideously Important Voltage-Current Graphs

V-I graphs show how the current varies as you change the voltage. Learn these four real well:

Resistor
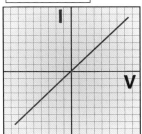
The current through a **RESISTOR** (at constant temperature) is _proportional to voltage_.

Different Wires
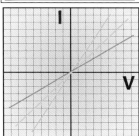
Different wires have different _resistances_, hence the different _slopes_.

Filament Lamp
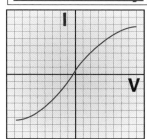
As the _temperature_ of the filament _increases_, the _resistance also increases_, hence the _curve_.

Diode
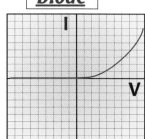
Current will only flow through a diode _in one direction_, as shown.

In the end, you'll have to learn this — resistance is futile...
There are quite a lot of important details on this page and you need to _learn all of them_. The only way to make sure you really know it is to _cover up the page_ and see how much of it you can _scribble down_ from _memory_. Sure, it's not that easy — but it's the only way. Enjoy.

SECTION ONE — ELECTRICITY AND MAGNETISM

Circuit Symbols and Devices

You have to know all these circuit symbols for the Exam. Hey, I know — learn them now!

Circuit Symbols You Should Know:

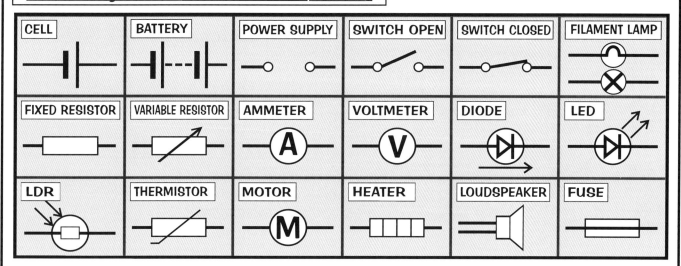

CELL	BATTERY	POWER SUPPLY	SWITCH OPEN	SWITCH CLOSED	FILAMENT LAMP
FIXED RESISTOR	VARIABLE RESISTOR	AMMETER	VOLTMETER	DIODE	LED
LDR	THERMISTOR	MOTOR	HEATER	LOUDSPEAKER	FUSE

1) Variable Resistor

1) A _resistor_ whose resistance can be _changed_ by twiddling a knob or something.
2) The old-fashioned ones are _huge coils of wire_ with a _slider_ on them.
3) They're great for _altering the current_ flowing through a circuit.
   Turn the resistance _up_, the current _drops_.
   Turn the resistance _down_, the current goes _up_.

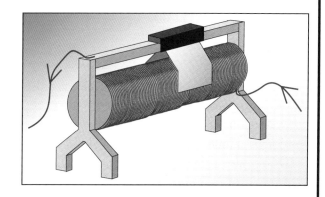

2) "Semiconductor Diode" or just "Diode"

1) A special device made from _semiconductor_ material such as _silicon_.
2) It lets current flow freely through it _in one direction_, but _not_ in the other (i.e. there's a very high resistance in the _reverse_ direction).
3) This turns out to be real useful in various _electronic circuits_.

3) Light Emitting Diode or "LED" to you

1) A diode which _gives out light_. It only lets current go through in _one direction_.

2) When it does pass current, it gives out a pretty _red_ or _green_ or _yellow_ light.

3) Stereos usually have lots of jolly little LEDs which _light up_ as the music's playing.

"Diode" — wasn't that a film starring Bruce Willis...

Another page of basic but important details about electrical circuits. You need to know all those circuit symbols as well as the extra details for the three special devices. When you think you know it all try _covering the page_ and _scribbling it all down_. See how you did, and _then try again_.

Series Circuits

You need to be able to tell the difference between series and parallel circuits _just by looking at them_. You also need to know the _rules_ about what happens with both types. Read on.

Series Circuits — all or nothing

1) In _series circuits_, the different components are connected _in a line_, _end to end_, between the +ve and −ve of the power supply (except for _voltmeters_, which are always connected _in parallel_, but they don't count as part of the circuit).
2) If you remove or disconnect _one_ component, the circuit is _broken_ and they all _stop_.
3) This is generally _not very handy_, and in practice, _very few things_ are connected in series.

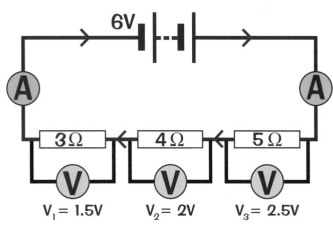

Voltages add to equal the _supply_: 1.5+2+2.5=6V
Total resistance = 3+4+5 = 12 Ohms
Current =V/R = 6/12 = 0.5A

In Series Circuits:

1) The _total resistance_ is just the _sum_ of all the resistances.
2) The _same current_ flows through _all parts_ of the circuit.
3) The _size of the current_ is determined by the _total Pd of the cells_ and the _total resistance_ of the circuit: i.e. I = V/R.
4) The _total Pd_ of the _supply_ is _shared_ between the various _components_, so the _voltages_ round a series circuit _always add up_ to equal the _source voltage_.
5) The _bigger_ the _resistance_ of a component, the bigger its _share_ of the _total Pd_.

Connection of Voltmeters and Ammeters

1) _Voltmeters_ are always connected _in parallel_ around components.
   In a _series circuit_, you can put voltmeters _around each component_. The readings from all the components will _add up_ to equal the reading from the _voltage source_. Simple, so learn it.
2) _Ammeters_ can be placed _anywhere_ in a _series circuit_ and will **ALL GIVE THE SAME READING**.

Christmas Fairy Lights are Wired in Series

Christmas fairy lights are about the _only real-life example_ of things connected in _series_, and we all know what a _pain_ they are when the _whole lot go out_ just because _one_ of the bulbs is slightly dicky.
The only _advantage_ is that the bulbs can be _very small_ because the total 230V is _shared out between them_, so _each bulb_ only has a _small voltage_ across it.

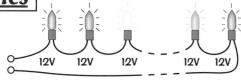

By contrast a string of lights as used on say a _building site_ are connected in _parallel_ so that each bulb receives the _full 230V_. If _one_ is removed, _the rest stay lit_ which is most _convenient_.

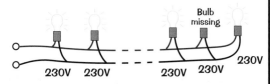

Make sure you know the _difference_ between these two wiring diagrams.

Series Circuits — phew, it's just one thing after another...

They really do want you to know the difference between series and parallel circuits. It's not that tricky but you do have to make a real effort to _learn all the details_. That's what this page is for. Learn all those details, then _cover the page_ and _scribble them all down_. Then try again...

Parallel Circuits

Parallel circuits are much more _sensible_ than series circuits and so they're _much more common_ in _real life_.

Parallel Circuits — Independence and Isolation

1) In _parallel circuits_, each component is _separately connected_ to the +ve and −ve of the _supply_.
2) If you remove or disconnect _one_ of them, it will _hardly affect the others at all_.
3) This is _obviously_ how _most things_ must be connected, for example in _cars_ and in _household electrics_. You have to be able to switch everything on and off _separately_.

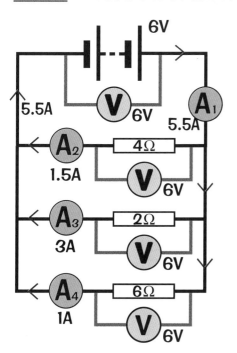

In Parallel Circuits:

1) _All components_ get the _full source Pd_, so the voltage is the _same_ across all components.
2) The _current_ through each component _depends on its resistance_.
   The _lower_ the resistance, the _bigger_ the current that'll flow through it.
3) The _total current_ flowing around the circuit is equal to the _total_ of all the currents in the _separate branches_.
4) In a parallel circuit, there are _junctions_ where the current either _splits_ or _rejoins_. The total current going _into_ a junction _always equals_ the total currents _leaving_ — fairly obviously.
5) The _total resistance_ of the circuit is _tricky to work out_, but it's _always LESS_ than the branch with the _smallest resistance_.

Voltages all equal to _supply voltage_: =6V
Total R is _less than_ the _smallest_, i.e. _less than_ 2Ω
Total Current (A₁) = _sum_ of all branches = A₂+A₃+A₄

Connection of Voltmeters and Ammeters

1) Once again the _voltmeters_ are always connected _in parallel_ around components.
2) _Ammeters_ can be placed _in each branch_ to measure the _different currents_ flowing through each branch, as well as _one near the supply_ to measure the _total current_ flowing out of it.

Everything Electrical in a Car is Connected in Parallel

Parallel connection is _essential_ in a car to give these _two features_:

> 1) Everything can be _turned on and off separately_.
> 2) Everything always gets the _full voltage_ from the battery.

The only _slight effect_ is that when you turn _lots of things on_ the lights may go _dim_ because the battery can't provide _full voltage_ under _heavy load_. This is normally a _very slight_ effect. You can spot the same thing at home when you turn a kettle on, if you watch very carefully.

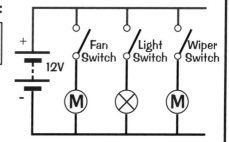

Electric Circuits — unparalleled dreariness...

Make sure you can scribble down a parallel circuit and know what the advantages are. Learn the five numbered points and the details for connecting ammeters and voltmeters, and also what two features make parallel connection essential in a car. Then _cover the page_ and _scribble it_...

8

Static Electricity

Static electricity is all about charges which are _NOT_ free to move. This causes them to build up in one place and it often ends with a _spark_ or a _shock_ when they do finally move.

1) Build up of Static is Caused by Friction

1) When two _insulating_ materials are _rubbed together_, electrons will be _scraped off one_ and _dumped on the other_.
2) This'll leave a _positive static charge_ on one and a _negative_ static charge on the other.
3) _Which way_ the electrons are transferred _depends_ on the _two materials_ involved.
4) The classic examples are _polythene_ and _acetate_ rods being rubbed with a _cloth duster_, as shown in the diagrams:

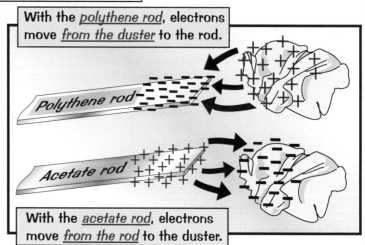

With the _polythene rod_, electrons move _from the duster_ to the rod.

With the _acetate rod_, electrons move _from the rod_ to the duster.

2) Only Electrons Move — Never the Positive Charges

Watch out for this in Exams. Both +ve and –ve electrostatic charges are only ever produced by the _movement of electrons_. The positive charges _definitely do not move_! A positive static charge is always caused by electrons _moving away elsewhere_, as shown above. Don't forget!

3) Like Charges Repel, Opposite Charges Attract

1) This is _easy_ and, I'd have thought, _kind of obvious_.
2) Two things with _opposite electric charges_ are _attracted_ to each other.
3) Two things with the _same electric charge_ will _repel_ each other.
4) These _forces get weaker_ the _further apart_ the two things are — pretty obviously.

4) As Charge Builds Up, So Does the Voltage — Causing Sparks

1) The _greater the CHARGE_ on an _isolated_ object, the _greater the VOLTAGE_ between it and the Earth.
2) If the voltage gets _big enough_ there's a _spark_ which _jumps across_ the gap.

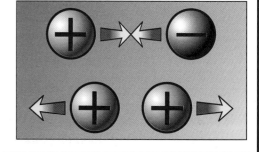

'ZAP!'

3) High voltage cables can be _dangerous_ for this reason.
4) Big sparks have been known to _leap_ from _overhead cables_ to earth. But not often.
5) A charged conductor can be _discharged safely_ by connecting it to earth with a _metal strap_.

Phew — it's enough to make your hair stand on end...

The way to tackle this page is to first _learn the four headings_ till you can _scribble them all down_. Then learn the details for each one, and keep practising by _covering the page_ and scribbling down each heading with as many details as you can remember for each one. Just _keep trying_...

Static Electricity — Examples

They like asking you to give *quite detailed examples* in Exams. Make sure you *learn all these details*.

Static Electricity Being Helpful:

1) Spray Painting:

1) The *spray nozzle* is connected to a *+ve terminal*.
2) This makes all the spray drops *positively charged*.
3) This makes them *repel each other* and *spread out*.
4) The car being sprayed is connected to *earth* (or –ve), so the droplets are *attracted* to it.
5) A magnificent paint job is the result.

2) Dust Removal in Chimneys:

1) Just put a set of *charged plates* in a *chimney* or extractor duct and the particles of smoke or dust will be *attracted* to them.
2) Every now and then you *turn off* the electricity and *shake the dust into a bag* — easy peasy. These are known as *electrostatic smoke precipitators*.

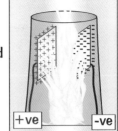

+ve   -ve

3) And Photocopiers... make use of static charge to *attract black toner* to just where it's wanted.

Static Electricity Being a Little Joker:

1) Car Shocks

Air rushing past your car can give it a *+ve charge*. When you get out and touch the *door* it gives you a real buzz — in the Exam make sure you say "*electrons* flow from earth, through you, to *neutralise* the +ve charge on the car". Some cars have *conducting rubber strips* which hang down behind the car. This gives a *safe discharge* to earth, but spoils all the fun.

2) Clothing Crackles

When *synthetic clothes* are *dragged* over each other (like in a *tumble drier*) or over your *head*, electrons get scraped off, leaving *static charges* on both parts, and that leads to the inevitable — *forces of attraction* (i.e. they stick together) and little *sparks/shocks* as the charges *rearrange themselves*.

Static Electricity Playing at Terrorist:

1) Lightning

Rain droplets fall to Earth with *positive charge*. This creates a *huge voltage* and a *big spark*.

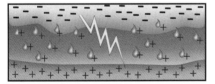

2) Grain Shoots, Paper Rollers and The Fuel Filling Nightmare:

1) As *fuel* flows out of a *filler pipe*, or *paper* drags over *rollers*, or *grain* shoots out of *pipes*, then *static can build up*.
2) This can easily lead to a *SPARK* and in *dusty* or *fumey* places — *BOOM!*
3) *The solution*: make the nozzles or rollers out of *METAL* so that the charge is *conducted away*, instead of building up.
4) It's also good to have *earthing straps* between the *fuel tank* and the *fuel pipe*, as shown on the diagram:

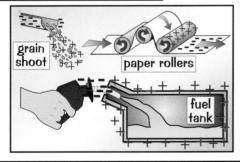

grain shoot

paper rollers

fuel tank

Static Electricity — learn the shocking truth...

This page is nicely broken up into three main sections with two subsections in each. This makes it quite a bit easier to learn. First learn the main headings, then the subheadings and then all the details that go with each. Slowly you *build it all up* in your head till you can *scribble it all down*.

Mains Electricity — Hazards and Plugs

Now then, did you know... electricity is dangerous. It can kill you. Well just watch out for it, that's all.

Hazards in The Home — Eliminate Them before They Eliminate You

A _likely Exam question_ will show you a picture of domestic bliss but with various _electrical hazards_ in the picture such as kids shoving their fingers into sockets and stuff like that, and they'll ask you to _list all the hazards_. This should be mostly _common sense_, but it won't half help if you've already learnt this list:

1) _Long cables_ or _frayed cables_.
2) _Cables_ in contact with something _hot_ or _wet_.
3) Pet rabbits or _children_ (always hazardous).
4) _Water near sockets_, or _shoving_ things into sockets.
5) _Damaged plugs_, or _too many_ plugs into one socket.
6) Lighting sockets _without bulbs in_.
7) Appliances without their _covers_ on.

Plugs and Cables — Learn the Safety Features

Hey, wow, look! — some stuff you can actually use in your everyday life. Phew.

First of All — Get the Wiring Right:

1) The _right coloured wire_ to each pin, and _firmly screwed_ in.
2) _No bare wires_ showing inside the plug.
3) _Cable grip_ tightly fastened over the cable _outer layer_.

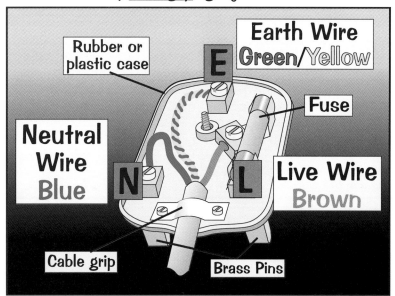

Rubber or plastic case

Earth Wire Green/Yellow

E

Fuse

Neutral Wire Blue

N

L

Live Wire Brown

Cable grip

Brass Pins

Important Plug Features:

1) The _metal parts_ are made of _copper or brass_ because these are _very good conductors_.
2) The case, cable grip and cable insulation are all made of _plastic_ because this is a really good _insulator_ and is _flexible_ too.
3) This all keeps the electricity flowing _where it should_.

Some people are so careless with electricity — it's shocking...

Make sure you can list all those hazards in the home and make sure you know all the details for wiring a plug. In particular, make sure you know exactly what each coloured wire is _called_ and exactly where it goes. Learnt it all? Good-O. So _cover the page_ and _scribble it all down again_.

Mains Electricity — Earthing and Fuses

Earthing and Fuses Prevent Fires and Shocks

1) The LIVE WIRE alternates between a HIGH +VE AND −VE VOLTAGE, with an average of 230V.
2) The NEUTRAL WIRE is always at OV.
3) *NORMALLY*, electricity flows in and out through the *live and neutral* wires *only*.
4) The E R H I E and *fuse* (or circuit breaker) are just for *safety* and *work together* like this:

1) If a *fault* develops in which the *live* somehow touches the *metal case*, then because the case is *earthed*, a *big current* flows in through the *live*, through the *case* and out down the *earth wire*.

2) This *surge* in current *blows the fuse* (or trips the circuit breaker), which *cuts off* the *live supply*.

3) This *isolates* the *whole appliance* making it *impossible* to get an electric *shock* from the case. It also prevents the risk of *fire* caused by the heating effect of a large current.

4) *Fuses* should be *rated* as near as possible but *just higher* than the *normal operating current* (see below).

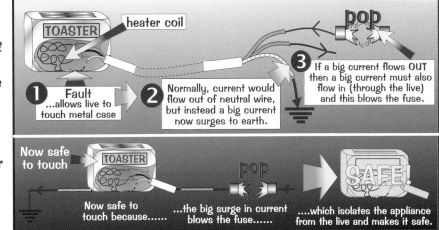

"Double Insulation" Just Means it Has a Plastic Outer Case

1) All appliances with *metal cases* must be "*earthed*" to avoid the danger of *electric shock*.
2) "Earthing" just means the metal case must be *attached to the earth wire* in the cable.
3) If the appliance has a *plastic casing* and no metal parts *showing* then it's said to be *DOUBLE INSULATED*.
4) Anything with *double insulation* like that *doesn't need an earth wire*, just a live and neutral.

Calculating Fuse Ratings — Always Use the Formula: "P=VI"

1) Most *electrical goods* indicate their *power rating* and *voltage rating*.
2) To work out the *FUSE* needed, you simply need to work out the *current* that the item will *normally* use.
3) That means using the formula "*P=VI*", or rather, "*I=P/V*", which you get using the triangle.

EXAMPLE 1 : A dinky little knuckle scrubber is rated at 240V, 700W. Find the fuse needed.
ANSWER: I = P/V = 700/240 = 2.9A. Normally, the fuse should be rated just a little higher than the normal current, so a 3 amp or 5 amp fuse is ideal for this one.

EXAMPLE 2: A hairdrier is rated at 240V, 1.1kW. Find the fuse needed.
ANSWER: I = P/V =1100/240 = 4.6A. The fuse should be rated just a little higher than the normal current, so a 5 amp fuse is ideal for this one.

Learn about Earthing — but don't blow a fuse...

Make sure you know which wire is the dangerous one, and which two wires normally carry the current. Trickiest of all, make sure you understand how earthing and fuses act together to make things safe. Earthing is quite complicated, but you *can* understand it. *Learn and scribble.*

The Cost of Domestic Electricity

Electricity is by far the *most useful* form of energy. Compared to gas or oil or coal etc. it's *much easier* to turn it into the *four main types* of useful energy: *Heat, light, sound* and *motion*.

Reading Your Electricity Meter and Working out the Bill

Yip, this is in the syllabus. Don't ask me why, because you never actually need to bother in real life!

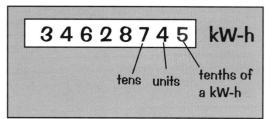

| 3 4 6 2 8 7 4 5 | kW-h |

tens   units   tenths of a kW-h

The reading on your meter shows the *total number of units* (kW-h) used since the meter was fitted. Each bill is worked out from the *INCREASE* in the meter reading since it was *last read* for the previous bill.

You need to *study* this bill until you know what all the different bits *are for*, and how it all works out. They could give you one *very similar* in the Exam.

Electricity Bill

Previous meter reading............345412.3
This meter reading...................346287.5
Number of units used......................875.2

Cost per unit......................................6.3p
Cost of electricity used...................£55.14p
(875.2 units × 6.3p)
Fixed Quarterly charge......................£7.50
Total Bill..£62.64
VAT @ 8%..£5.01
Final total...**£67.65**

Kilowatt-hours (kW-h) are "UNITS" of Energy

1) Your electricity meter counts the number of *"UNITS"* used.
2) A *"UNIT"* is otherwise known as a *kilowatt-hour*, or *kW-h*.
3) A "*kW-h*" might sound like a unit of power, but it's not — it's an *amount of energy*.

> A *KILOWATT-HOUR* is the amount of electrical energy used by a *1 KW APPLIANCE* left on for *1 HOUR*.

4) Make sure you can turn *1 kW-h* into *3,600,000 Joules* like this:
"E=P×t" =1kW × 1 hour =1000W × 3,600 secs = **3,600,000J**   (=3.6MJ)
(The formula is "Energy = Power×time", and the units must be converted to SI first.   See P. 13, 14 and 15)

The Two Easy Formulae for Calculating The Cost of Electricity

These must surely be the two most *trivial and obvious* formulae you'll ever see:

No. of *UNITS* (kW-h) used = *POWER* (in kW) × *TIME* (in hours)	Units = kW × hours
COST = No. of *UNITS* × *PRICE* per UNIT	Cost = Units × Price

EXAMPLE: Find the cost of leaving a 60W light bulb on for a) 30 minutes   b) one year.
ANSWER: a) *No. of UNITS = kW × hours* = 0.06kW × ½hr = 0.03 units.
   Cost = UNITS × price per UNIT(6.3p)   = 0.03 × 6.3p = **0.189p** for 30 mins.

   b) *No. of UNITS = kW × hours* = 0.06kW × (24×365)hr = 525.6 units.
   Cost = UNITS × price per UNIT(6.3p)   = 525.6 × 6.3p = **£33.11** for one year.

N.B.   Always turn the *power* into *kW* (not Watts) and the *time* into *hours* (not minutes)

Kilowa Towers — the Best Lit Hotel in Hawaii...

This page has three sections and you need to learn the stuff in all of them. Start by memorising the headings, then learn the details under each heading. Then *cover the page* and *scribble down* what you know. Check back and see what you missed, and then *try again*. And keep trying.

Symbols, Units and Formulae

This is all very basic stuff and you need to learn it all pretty thoroughly. If you don't, and you then try and do other Physics, it's like trying to write stories without learning the alphabet first. So as long as this is all just a load of weird symbols and nonsense to you then you won't find Physics very easy at all. This is the Physics alphabet and without it you're... in trouble.

	Quantity	Symbol	Standard Units	Formula
1	Potential Difference	V	Volts, V	$V = I \times R$
2	Current	I	Amperes, A	$I = V / R$
3	Resistance	R	Ohms, Ω	$R = V / I$
4	Charge	Q	Coulombs, C	
5	Power	P	Watts, W	$P = V \times I$
6	Energy	E	Joules, J	$E = P \times t$
7	Time	t	Seconds, s	(or $E = V \times I \times t$)
8	Force	F	Newtons, N	
9	Mass	m	Kilograms, kg	
10	Weight (a force)	W	Newtons, N	$W = mg$
11	Density	D	kg per m^3, kg/m^3	$D = m/V$
12	Moment	M	Newton-metres, Nm	$M = F \times r$
13	Velocity or Speed	v or s	metres/sec, m/s	$s = d/t$
14	Acceleration	a	metres/sec^2, m/s^2	$a = \Delta v/t$
15	Pressure	P	Pascals, Pa (N/m^2)	$P = F/A$
16	Area	A	metres^2, m^2	
17	Volume	V	metres^3, m^3	
18	Frequency	f	Hertz, Hz	
19	Wavelength (a distance)	λ or d	metres, m	
20	Work done	Wd	Joules, J	$Wd = F \times d$
21	Potential Energy	PE	Joules, J	
22	Kinetic Energy	KE	Joules, J	

There's also *efficiency*, which has no units:

$$\text{Efficiency} = \frac{\text{Useful work output}}{\text{Total energy input}}$$

Physics — isn't it just wonderful...

Your task is *simplicity itself*. Leave the "Quantity" column exposed and cover up the other three. Then simply *fill in the three columns* for each quantity: "Symbol", "Units", "Formula". And *just keep practising and practising till you can do it all*. This really is so important. So do it.

SECTION ONE — ELECTRICITY AND MAGNETISM

14

Using Formulae

Formulae aren't so bad — it's Always the Same Old Routine

1) The thing about using formulae in Physics is that it's _always the same old routine_.
2) Once you've learnt how to do it for _one_ formula, you can do it for _any other_.
3) And that makes the whole thing _real simple_.
4) Mind you there's still a lot of people out there who seem to make a real meal of it.
5) Let's take it nice and slowly...

Formula Triangles are Pretty Useful for Getting it Right

1) _ALL_ the formulae that you'll come across in Physics can easily be put into _formula triangles_.
2) It's _pretty important_ to learn how to put _any formula_ into a triangle.
3) There are _two nice easy rules_:

> 1) If the formula is "<u>A = B×C</u>"
>   then _A goes on the top_ and _B×C goes on the bottom_.
>
> 2) If the formula is "<u>A = B/C</u>"
>   then _B must go on the top_ (because that's the only way it'll give "B divided by something"), and so pretty obviously _A and C must go on the bottom_.

Three Jolly Examples of Putting Formulas into Formula Triangles:

V=I×R
turns into:

W=mg
turns into:

P=F/A
turns into:

Using Formulae — The Five Easy Rules

1) _FIND THE RIGHT FORMULA_ which contains _THE THING YOU WANT TO FIND_ together with the _OTHER TWO THINGS_ which you are given _VALUES_ for.

2) _CONVERT_ that formula into a _FORMULA TRIANGLE_.

3) _STICK_ the numbers in — and _WORK OUT_ the answer.

4) _THINK VERY CAREFULLY_ about all the _UNITS_.

5) _CHECK_ that the answer is _SENSIBLE_.

Formulae — aren't they just fabulous...

Physics formulae are _very repetitive_. You really must get it into your head that they're _basically all the same_. This page has the _simple rules_ that would allow _anyone_ to work out the answers without really knowing anything about Physics at all. On the next page we'll do some examples, but first... _learn these rules_. Keep trying until you can _cover the page_ and _scribble them down_.

Using Formulae — An Example

A Nice Easy Example to Illustrate the Method:

EXAMPLE: *A Giant Moon Hamster has a mass of 130kg. Find its weight on the Moon where the value for "g" is 1.6N/kg.*

ANSWER:

1) *FIND THE FORMULA*.

The *three things* mentioned are: *mass*, *weight* and *"g"*.
That should instantly make you think of the formula: *W=mg*.

2) *NOW CONVERT IT INTO A FORMULA TRIANGLE*:

W=mg means W=m×g, so the triangle is:

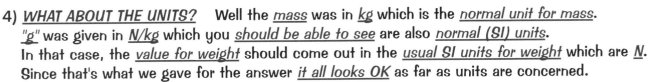

3) We want to *find weight*, so *COVER UP W*.

That leaves *m×g showing* — so we have: W = m×g = 130 × 1.6 = <u>208N</u>
And there it is — *the answer*. Easy huh!   Now just *two important formalities*:

4) *WHAT ABOUT THE UNITS?*   Well the *mass* was in *kg* which is the *normal unit for mass*.
"g" was given in *N/kg* which you *should be able to see* are also *normal (SI) units*.
In that case, the *value for weight* should come out in the *usual SI units for weight* which are *N*.
Since that's what we gave for the answer *it all looks OK* as far as units are concerned.

5) *IS THE ANSWER SENSIBLE?*   Well that's *not always easy* to tell.
In this case though you should be able to *agree* that 208N *isn't miles too big* and it *isn't miles too small*. So yeah, from that point of view it's *pretty sensible*.
Answers like 208,000N or 0.00208N would make you worry a bit really, I'd hope — and then
you'd *go back and check* your working out, to see if you'd done something *silly*. Wouldn't you!

And Finally — Watch out For the Units

Once you've got the hang of formula triangles there's really only one thing left to get wrong, and that's *UNITS*.   There's *two things* about units that you have to really watch out for:

1) Make sure that the numbers *you put IN* to the formula are in *STANDARD (SI) UNITS*.
2) When you write the answer down, make sure your *answer* has its *proper units*.

FOUR IMPORTANT EXAMPLES:

500g must be turned into *0.5kg*,
4 minutes must be turned into *240 seconds*,
700kJ must be turned into *700,000J*,
145cm must be turned into *1.45m*.

1) And the same goes for *all the other units*.
2) You need to make sure they're in *SI units* before putting them *into a formula*.
3) The *big exception* to that is *areas in cm²* when working out pressure. (See P. 36, 37)
4) If you don't put SI units *in* then the answer won't come *out* with SI units — and that can get tricky unless you know what you're doing. And let's face it, you probably don't.   *SI units then*.

Yah — "Absolutely Fabulous"

Phew. There it is then. The *Fool-proof Five Step Method* for doing formulae questions.
D'ya reckon you've got it sussed? Yeah? OK — try these, and then we'll all know — won't we.
1) The combined mass of an astronaut and a lunatic Moon Hamster is 212kg. Find the weight.
2) A 6 Volt battery supplies a current of 2A through a resistor. Find the value of the resistor.
3) Find the work done when a force of 20N acts through a distance of 5.3m.
4) Find the pressure when a force of 500N pushes on an area of 50cm².

Magnetic Fields

There's a proper definition of a _magnetic field_ which you really ought to learn:

> A _MAGNETIC FIELD_ is a region where _MAGNETIC MATERIALS_ (like iron and steel) and also _WIRES CARRYING CURRENTS_ experience _A FORCE_ acting on them.

Learn all These _Magnetic Field Diagrams, Arrow-perfect_

They're real likely to give you one of these diagrams to do in your Exam.
So make sure you know them, especially _which way the arrows point_ — _ALWAYS from N to S!_

Bar Magnet

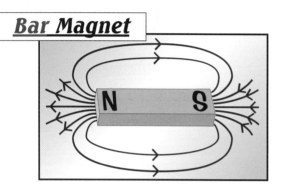

Solenoid

Same field as a bar magnet _outside_.

Strong and uniform field on the _inside_.

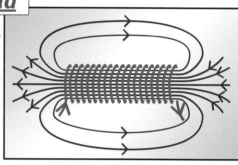

Two Bar Magnets _Attracting_

Opposite poles ATTRACT, as I'm sure you know.

Two Bar Magnets _Repelling_

Like poles REPEL, as you must surely know.

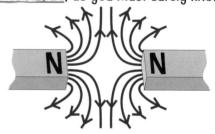

The Earth's Magnetic Field

Note that the _magnetic poles_ are _opposite_ to the _Geographic Poles_, i.e. the _south pole_ is at the _North Pole_ — if you see what I mean!

The Magnetic Field Round a Current-carrying Wire

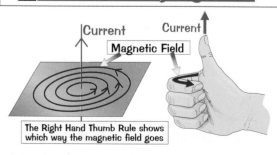

The Right Hand Thumb Rule shows which way the magnetic field goes

Magnetic fields — there's no getting away from them...

Mmm, this is a nice easy page for you isn't it. Learn the definition of what a magnetic field is and the six field diagrams. Make sure you know which way all the arrows go and which way the magnetic poles are compared to the Earth. Then _cover the page_ and _scribble it all down_.

Magnetic Materials

Only Iron, Steel and Nickel are Magnetic

Don't forget that _all_ other _common metals_ are _NOT magnetic at all_. So a magnet _won't stick_ to _aluminium ladders_ or _copper kettles_ or _brass trumpets_ or _gold rings_ or _silver spoons_.

Iron is Magnetically "Soft" — Ideal for Electromagnets

1) In magnetic terms, _"soft"_ means it _changes easily_ between being _magnetised_ and _demagnetised_.
2) Iron is "soft" which makes it perfect for _electromagnets_ which need to be _turned on and off_.

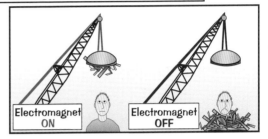

Electromagnet ON   Electromagnet OFF

Steel is Magnetically "Hard" — Ideal for Permanent Magnets

1) Magnetically _"hard"_ means that the material _retains_ its magnetism.
2) This would be _hopeless_ in an _electromagnet_, but is exactly what's required for _permanent magnets_. Steel _retains its magnetism_, so we call it a magnetically _"hard"_ material.

To MAGNETISE a Piece of Steel, etc:

1) Put it in a _solenoid_ with a _steady DC supply_.
2) Turn _off_ the current, _pull it out_, and there it is, a _permanent magnet_.

Magnetising - D.C. SUPPLY

Direct current   S   N

To DEMAGNETISE a Piece of Steel, etc:

1) Put it in a _solenoid_ with an _AC supply_.
2) Then _pull it out_ with the _AC current still going_ and there it is, _demagnetised_.

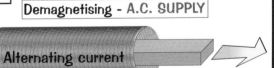

Demagnetising - A.C. SUPPLY

Alternating current

A Plotting Compass is a Freely Suspended Magnet

1) This means it always _aligns itself_ with the _magnetic field_ that it's in.
2) This is great for plotting _magnetic field lines_ like around the _bar magnets_ shown above.
3) Away from any magnets, it will _align_ with the magnetic field of the _Earth_ and point _North_.
4) _Any magnet_ suspended so it can turn _freely_ will also come to rest pointing _North-South_.

Learn about Magnets — it'll save you coming unstuck...

There you go, six nice easy headings, a few jolly pictures and a smattering of drivelly details. All you've gotta do is gently pummel them into your memory. What's that? Have I got any suggestions? Sure. Try _covering the page_ and _scribbling it all down_, _check it_ and then _try again_.

Electromagnets

An Electromagnet is just a Coil of Wire with an Iron Core

1) _Electromagnets_ are _really simple_.
2) They're simply a _solenoid_ (which is just a _coil of wire_) with a piece of _"soft"_ iron inside.
3) When _current flows_ through the _wires_ of the solenoid it creates a _magnetic field_ around it.
4) The _soft iron core_ has the effect of _increasing_ the _magnetic field strength_.

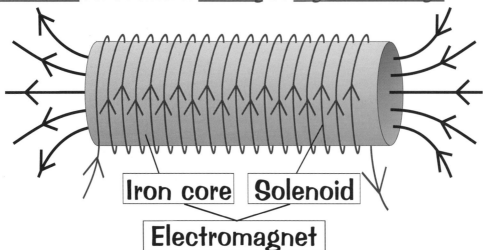

Iron core Solenoid

Electromagnet

1) The _magnetic field_ around an _electromagnet_ is just like the one round a _bar magnet_, only _stronger_.
2) This means that the _ends_ of a _solenoid_ act like the _North Pole_ and _South Pole_ of a bar magnet.
3) Pretty obviously, if the direction of the _current_ is _reversed_, the N and S poles will _swap ends_.

The _STRENGTH_ of an _ELECTROMAGNET_ depends on _THREE FACTORS:_	1) The size of the _CURRENT_. 2) The number of _TURNS_ the coil has. 3) What the _CORE_ is made of.

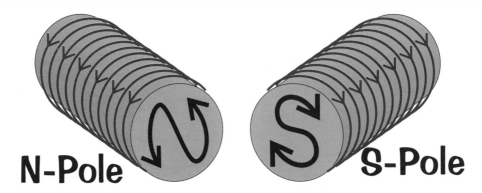

N-Pole   S-Pole

If you imagine looking directly into one end of a solenoid, the _direction of current flow_ tells you
whether it's the _N or S pole_ you're looking at, as shown by the _two diagrams_ above.
You need to remember those diagrams.
They may show you a solenoid _in the Exam_ and ask you which pole it is you're looking at.

Electromagnets really irritate me — I just get solenoid with them...

This is all very basic information, and quite easy to remember I'd have thought. Learn the
heading and the diagrams first, then _cover the page_ and _scribble them down_. Then gradually fill
in the other details. _Keep looking back and checking_. Try to learn _all_ the points. Lovely innit.

Electromagnetic Devices

Electromagnets always have a _soft iron core_, which _increases the strength_ of the magnet. The core has to be _soft_ (magnetically soft, that is), so that when the _current_ is turned _off_, the magnetism _disappears_ with it. The four applications below all depend on that happening.

The Scrapyard Electromagnet

1) The electromagnet consists of a _big coil of wire_, with _many turns_, and a _soft iron core_.
2) With the current _on_, this creates a _very strong magnetic field_, which _attracts_ the scrap iron.

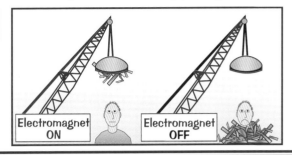

Electromagnet ON   Electromagnet OFF

The Circuit Breaker — or Resettable Fuse

1) This is placed on the _incoming live wire_.
2) If the current gets _too high_, the _magnetic field_ in the coil _pulls_ the iron core which "_trips_" the switch and _breaks the circuit_.
3) It can be _reset_ manually, but will always flick itself off if the _current_ is _too high_.

The Old Dependable Relay — an Electromagnetic Switch

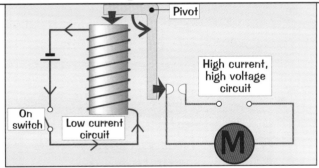

E.g. A very big relay is used in _cars_ for switching the _starter motor_, because it draws a _very big current_.

1) A _relay_ is a device which uses a _low current circuit_ to _switch_ a _high current circuit_ on/off.
2) When the switch in the low current circuit is _closed_ it turns the _electromagnet ON_ which _attracts_ the _iron rocker_.
3) The rocker _pivots_ and _closes the contacts_ in the high current circuit.
4) When the low current switch is _opened_, the electromagnet _stops pulling_, the rocker returns, and the _high current circuit_ is _broken_ again.

The Good Old Electric Bell

These are used in schools to stress everyone out.

1) When the switch is _closed_, the electromagnets are turned _on_.
2) They pull the _iron arm DOWN_ which _clangs_ the bell, but at the same time _breaks the contact_, which immediately _turns off_ the electromagnets.
3) The arm then _springs back_, which _closes_ the _contact_, and _off we go again_...
4) The whole sequence happens _very quickly_, maybe _10 times a second_, so the bell sounds like a continuous "_brrriiiinnngg_" sound. Nice.

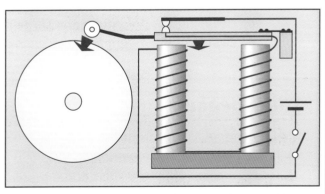

Watch out for relays — they can be a real turn-on...

They nearly always have one of these in the Exam. Usually it's a circuit diagram of one of them and likely as not they'll ask you to explain exactly how it works. Make sure you _learn all those tricky details_ for the three tricky ones. _Cover, scribble, etc..._

The Motor Effect

Anything *carrying a current* in a *magnetic field* will experience a *force*. There are *three important cases*:

A Current in a Magnetic Field Experiences a Force

1) The two tests shown here both demonstrate the *force* on a *current-carrying wire* placed in a *magnetic field*.
2) The *force* gets *bigger* if either the *current* or the *magnetic field* is made bigger.
3) Note that in *both cases* the *force* on the wire is at *90°* to both the *wire* and to the *magnetic field*.

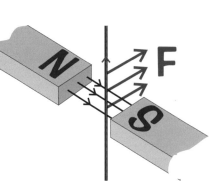

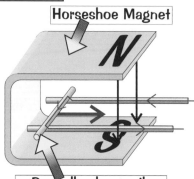

Horseshoe Magnet

Bar rolls along rails when current is applied

The Simple Electric Motor

1) The diagram shows the *forces* acting on the two *side arms* of the *coil*.
2) These forces are just the *usual forces* which act on *any current* in a *magnetic field*.

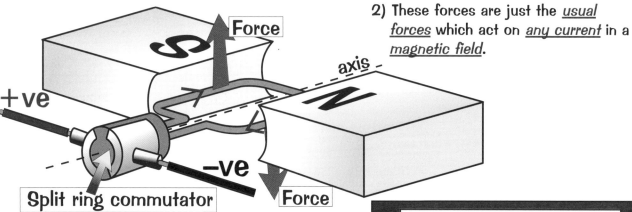

+ve

Force

axis

−ve

Force

Split ring commutator

3) Because the coil is on a *spindle* and the forces act *one up* and *one down*, it *rotates*.

4) The *direction of rotation* of the motor can be *reversed* by either:

    a) swapping the *polarity* of the *DC supply*,
    b) swapping the *magnetic poles* over.

The Four Factors Which Will Increase the Speed of The Motor

1) More *CURRENT*
2) More *TURNS* on the coil
3) *STRONGER MAGNETIC FIELD*
4) A *SOFT IRON CORE* in the coil

Loudspeakers Also Demonstrate the Motor Effect

1) *AC electrical signals* from the *amplifier* are fed to the *speaker coil* (shown red).
2) These make the coil move *back and forth* over the North pole of the *magnet*.
3) These movements make the *cardboard cone vibrate* and this creates *sounds*.

Learn about the motor effect — and feel the force...

Same old routine here. *Learn all the details*, diagrams and all, then *cover the page* and *scribble it all down* again *from memory*. I presume you do realise that you should be scribbling it down as scruffy as you like — because all you're trying to do is make sure that you really do *know it*.

Electromagnetic Induction

Sounds terrifying. Well sure it's quite mysterious, but it isn't that complicated:

ELECTROMAGNETIC INDUCTION: The creation of a **VOLTAGE** (and maybe current) in a wire which is experiencing a **CHANGE IN MAGNETIC FIELD**.

For some reason they use the word "*induction*" rather than "*creation*", but it amounts to the *same thing*.

EM Induction — a) Flux cutting   b) Field Through a Coil

Electromagnetic induction is the *induction* of a *voltage* and/or *current* in a conductor.
There are *two different situations* where you get *EM induction*. You need to know about *both* of them:
   a) The *conductor* moves across a *magnetic field* and "*cuts*" through the lines of *magnetic flux*.
   b) The *magnetic field* through a *closed coil* CHANGES, i.e. gets *bigger* or *smaller* or *reverses*.

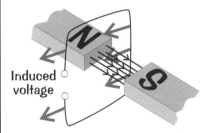
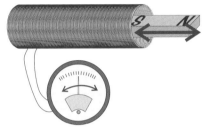
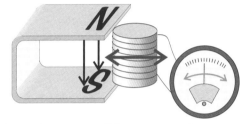

Induced voltage

If the direction of *movement* is *reversed*, then the induced *voltage/current* will be *reversed* too.

Generators and Dynamos

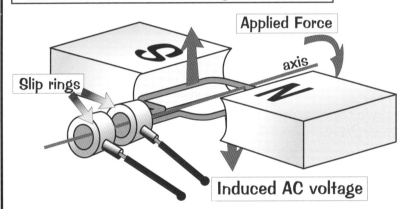

Applied Force

axis

Slip rings

Induced AC voltage

1) Generators *rotate a coil* in a *magnetic field*.
2) Their *construction* is pretty much like a *motor*.
3) The *difference* is the *slip rings* which means they produce *AC voltage*, as shown by these *CRO displays*:

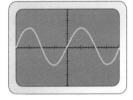
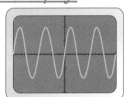

4) Note that *faster revs* produces not only *more peaks* on the CRO display but *higher overall voltage* too.

Three Factors Affect The Size of the Induced Voltage:

1) The **STRENGTH** of the **MAGNET**
2) The *number of TURNS* on the **COIL**
3) The **SPEED** of movement

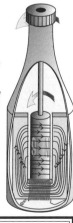

Dynamos are slightly different from *generators* because they rotate the *magnet*. This still causes the *field through the coil* to *swap* every half turn, so the output is *just the same*, as shown in the CRO displays above.

"The Rate of Change of Flux" — pretty tricky isn't it...

"Electromagnetic Induction" gets my vote for "Definitely Most Trickiest Topic in GCSE Double Science". If it wasn't so important maybe you wouldn't have to bother learning it. The trouble is this is how all our electricity is generated. So it's pretty important. *Learn and scribble...*

Transformers and The National Grid

Transformers use *Electromagnetic Induction*.   So they will *only* work on *AC*.

Transformers Change the Voltage — but only AC Voltages

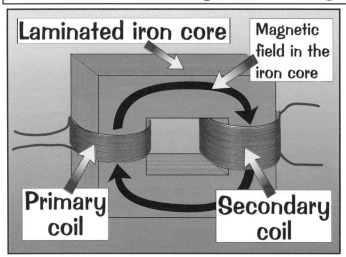

1) Transformers are used to *change voltage*. They can either *increase it* or *decrease it*.

   Step-up transformers step the voltage *up*. *Step-down* transformers step it *down*.

2) They work using *electromagnetic induction*.

3) The *laminated iron core* is purely for transferring the *magnetic field* from the primary coil to the secondary coil.

4) No *electricity* flows round the *iron core*, only *magnetic field*.

5) The iron core is *laminated* with *layers of insulation* to reduce the *eddy currents* which *heat it up*, and therefore *waste energy*.

The National Grid Carries Electricity

1) The *National Grid* is the *network* of pylons and cables which covers *the whole country*.

2) It takes electricity from the *power stations*, to just where it's needed in *homes* and *industry*.

3) It enables power to be *generated* anywhere on the grid, and to then be *supplied* anywhere else on the grid.   *Learn* all these features of the *NATIONAL GRID* — power stations, transformers, pylons, etc:

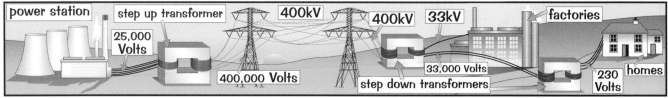

Pylon Cables are at 400,000V to keep the Current Low

You need to understand why the *VOLTAGE* is so *HIGH* and why it's *AC*.   Learn these points.

1) The formula for *power supplied* is: *Power = Voltage × Current* or: $P = V \times I$

2) So to transmit *a lot of power*, you either need *high voltage* or *high current*.

3) The problem with *high current* is the *loss* (as heat) caused by the *resistance* of the cables.

4) It's much *cheaper* to boost the voltage up to *400,000V* and keep the current *very low*.

5) This requires *transformers* as well as *big pylons* with *huge insulators*, but it's still *cheaper*.

6) The transformers have to *step* the voltage *up* at one end, for *efficient transmission*, and then bring it back down to *safe useable levels* at the other end.

7) This is why it has to be *AC* on the National Grid — so that the *transformers* will work!

400,000 Volts? — that could give you a buzz...

Quite a few tricky details on this page. Transformers sound quite scary but really they're not too bad. Just learn the simple facts. The National Grid is also easy enough, but fully explaining why pylon cables are at 400,000V is a bit trickier — but you do need to learn it.   *Scribble it.*

Revision Summary for Section One

Electricity and magnetism. What fun. This is definitely Physics at its most grisly. The big problem with Physics in general is that usually there's nothing to "see". You're told that there's a current flowing or a magnetic field lurking, but there's nothing you can actually see with your eyes. That's what makes it so difficult. To get to grips with Physics you have to get used to learning about things which you can't see. Try these questions and see how well you're doing.

1) Describe what current, voltage and resistance are, and compare them to a water circuit.
2) What carries current in metals? What's "conventional current" and what's the problem?
3) What do AC and DC stand for? Explain what they both mean. Sketch the CRO display for each.
4) What are the four types of energy which electricity can easily be converted into?
5) Sketch a circuit showing four devices converting energy. Describe all the energy changes.
6) Sketch out the standard test circuit with all the details. Describe how it's used.
7) Sketch the four standard V-I graphs and explain their shapes. How do you get R from them?
8) Scribble down 18 circuit symbols that you know, with their names of course.
9) Write down two facts about: a) a variable resistor   b) a diode   c) an LED.
10) Sketch a typical series circuit and say why it is a series circuit, not a parallel one.
11) State five rules about the current, voltage and resistance in a series circuit.
12) Give examples of lights wired in series and wired in parallel and explain the main differences.
13) Sketch a typical parallel circuit, showing voltmeter and ammeter positions.
14) State five rules about the current, voltage and resistance in a parallel circuit.
15) Draw a circuit diagram of part of a car's electrics, and explain why they are in parallel.
16) What is static electricity? What is nearly always the cause of it building up?
17) Which particles move when static builds up, and which ones don't?
18) Give *two* examples each of static being: a) helpful   b) a little joker   c) terrorist.
19) Write down seven electrical hazards in the home.
20) Sketch a properly wired plug. Explain fully how earthing and fuses work.
21) Sketch an electricity meter and explain exactly what the number on it represents.
22) What's a kilowatt-hour? What are the two easy formulae for finding the cost of electricity?
23) Look at the table on P. 13. Cover the last three columns and write down all the hidden details.
24) Explain how formula triangles work. What are the five rules for using any formula?
25) What are the two rules to remember about units? Give an example of each.
   a) Find the current when a resistance of 96Ω is connected to a battery of 12V.
   b) Find the pressure exerted by a force of 2500N concentrated onto 0.5 cm².
   c) Find the mass of an object with a weight of 374N on Earth (where g = 10 m/s²).
   d) Find the power output of a heater which provides 77kJ of heat energy in 4 mins.
   e) Find the voltage supplied to a hairdrier which draws 10 Amps and gives out 2.4kW.
   f) Calculate the fuse needed for a kettle rated at 2.2kW, 240V.
26) Sketch magnetic fields for: a) a bar magnet, b) a solenoid, c) two magnets attracting,
   d) two magnets repelling, e) the Earth's magnetic field, f) a current-carrying wire.
27) What is meant by magnetically hard and soft?
28) How do you a) magnetise a piece of steel   b) demagnetise a piece of steel?
29) What is an electromagnet made of? Explain how to decide on the polarity of the ends?
30) Sketch and give details of: a) scrapyard magnet, b) circuit breaker, c) relay, d) electric bell.
31) Sketch two demos of the motor effect.
32) Sketch the details of a simple electric motor and list the four factors which affect the speed of it.
33) Give the definition of electromagnetic induction. Sketch three cases where it happens.
34) Sketch a generator with all the details. Sketch the CRO output you get from it.
35) List the three factors which affect the size of the induced voltage.
36) Sketch a transformer, and highlight the main details. Explain what transformers are used for.
37) Sketch a typical power station, and the national grid and explain why it's at 400kV.

Mass, Weight and Gravity

Gravity is the Force of Attraction Between All Masses

Gravity attracts *all masses*, but you only notice it when one of the masses is *really really big*, i.e. a planet. Anything near a planet or star is *attracted* to it *very strongly*. This has *three important effects*:

1) It makes all things *accelerate towards the ground* (all with the *same acceleration*, *g*, which = *10 m/s²* on Earth).

2) It gives everything a *weight*.

3) It keeps *planets*, *moons* and *satellites* in their *orbits*. The orbit is a *balance* between the *forward motion* of the object and the force of gravity *pulling it inwards*.

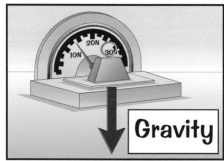

Gravity

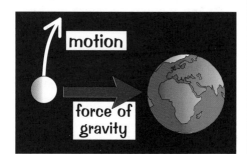

motion

force of gravity

Weight and Mass are Not the Same

To understand this you must *learn all these facts* about *mass and weight*.

1) *MASS* is the *AMOUNT OF MATTER* in an object. For any given object this will have *the same value ANYWHERE IN THE UNIVERSE*.

2) *WEIGHT* is caused by the *pull of gravity*. In most questions the *weight* of an object is just the *force of gravity* pulling it towards the centre of the *Earth*.

3) An object has the *same mass* whether it's on *Earth* or on the *Moon* — but its *weight* will be *different*. A 1 kg mass will *weigh LESS on the Moon* (1.6N) than it does on *Earth* (10N), simply because the *force of gravity* pulling on it is *less*.

4) *Weight is a force* measured in *Newtons*. *MASS* is *NOT* a force. It's measured in *kilograms*.

The Very Important Formula relating Mass, Weight and Gravity

$$W = m \times g$$

(Weight = mass × g)

1) Remember, *weight and mass are NOT the same*. Mass is in *kg*, weight is in *Newtons*.

2) The letter "*g*" represents the *strength of the gravity* and its value is *different* for *different planets*:

On Earth: g = 10 N/kg.
On the Moon: g is just 1.6 N/kg. That's because the *gravity is weaker*.

3) This formula is *hideously easy* to use:

EXAMPLE: What is the weight, in Newtons, of a 5kg mass, both on Earth and on the Moon?
Answer: "W = m × g". On Earth: W = 5 × 10 = *50N* (The weight of the 5kg mass is 50N)
On the Moon: W = 5 × 1.6 = *8N* (The weight of the 5kg mass is 8N)

See what I mean. Hideously easy — as long as you've learnt what all the letters mean.

Learn about gravity NOW — no point in "weighting" around...

Very often, the only way to "*understand*" something is to *learn all the facts about it*. That's certainly true here. "Understanding" the difference between mass and weight is no more than learning all those facts about them. When you've learnt all those facts, you'll understand it.

Force Diagrams

A _force_ is simply a _push_ or a _pull_. There are only _six different forces_ for you to know about:

> 1) _GRAVITY_ or _WEIGHT_ always acting _straight downwards_.
> 2) _REACTION FORCE_ from a _surface_, usually acting _straight upwards_.
> 3) _THRUST_ or _PUSH_ or _PULL_ due to an engine or rocket _speeding something up_.
> 4) _DRAG_ or _AIR RESISTANCE_ or _FRICTION_ which is _slowing the thing down_.
> 5) _LIFT_ due to an _aeroplane wing_.
> 6) _TENSION_ in a _rope_ or _cable_.

And there are basically only _FIVE DIFFERENT FORCE DIAGRAMS_ you can get:

1) Stationary Object — All Forces in Balance

1) The force of _GRAVITY_ (or weight) is acting _downwards_.
2) This causes a _REACTION FORCE_ from the surface _pushing_ the object _back up_.
3) This is the _only way_ it can be in _BALANCE_.
4) _Without_ a reaction force, it would _accelerate downwards_ due to the pull of gravity.
5) The two _HORIZONTAL forces_ must be _equal and opposite_ otherwise the object will _accelerate sideways_.

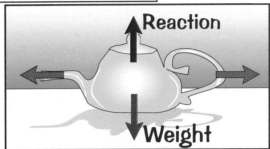

2) Steady Horizontal Velocity — All Forces in Balance!

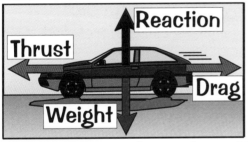

3) Steady Vertical Velocity — All Forces in Balance!

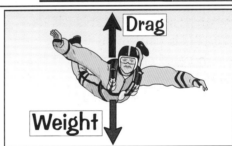

TAKE NOTE! To move with a _steady speed_ the forces must be in _BALANCE_. If there is an _unbalanced force_ then you get _ACCELERATION_, not steady speed. That's _rrrreal important_ so don't forget it.

4) Horizontal Acceleration — Unbalanced Forces

1) You only get _acceleration_ with an overall _resultant_ (unbalanced) _force_.
2) The _bigger_ this _unbalanced force_, the _greater_ the _acceleration_.

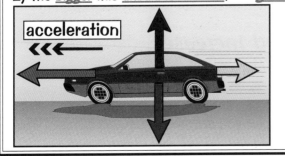

Note that the forces in the _other direction_ are still _balanced_.

5) Vertical Acceleration — Unbalanced Forces

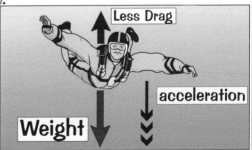

Revise Force Diagrams — but don't become unbalanced...

Make sure you learn those five different force diagrams. You'll almost certainly get one of them in your Exam. All you really need to remember is how the relative sizes of the arrows relate to the type of motion. It's pretty simple so long as you make the effort to _learn it_. So _scribble_...

Friction

Friction is Always There to Slow things Down

1) If an object has <u>no force</u> propelling it along it will always <u>slow down and stop</u> because of <u>friction</u>.
2) To travel at a <u>steady speed</u>, things always need a <u>driving force</u> to counteract the friction.
   Friction occurs in <u>THREE MAIN WAYS</u>:

Friction between Solid Surfaces which are Gripping

1) For example between <u>tyres and the road</u>.
2) There's always a <u>limit</u> as to how far two surfaces can <u>grip</u> each other, and if you demand <u>more force of friction</u> than they can manage, then they start to <u>slide</u> past each other instead.
3) In other words if you try to brake <u>too hard</u>, you'll <u>SKID</u>.

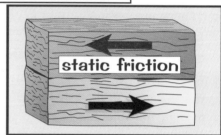
static friction

Friction between Surfaces which are Sliding Past Each Other

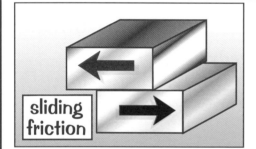
sliding friction

1) For example between <u>brake pads and brake discs</u>.
2) There's <u>just as much</u> force of <u>friction</u> here as between the tyres and the road.
3) In fact in the end, if you brake <u>hard enough</u> the friction here becomes <u>greater</u> than at the tyres, and then the wheel <u>skids</u>.

Resistance or "Drag" from Fluids (e.g. Air or Water)

1) The most important factor <u>by far</u> in <u>reducing drag in fluids (like air or water)</u> is keeping the shape of the object <u>streamlined</u>, like fish bodies or boat hulls or bird wings/bodies.
2) The <u>opposite extreme</u> is a <u>parachute</u> which is about as <u>high drag</u> as you can get — which is, of course, <u>the whole idea</u>.

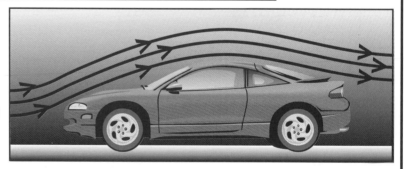

Friction Always Increases as the Speed Increases

1) A car has <u>much more friction</u> to <u>work against</u> when travelling at <u>60mph</u> compared to <u>30mph</u>.
2) So at 60mph the engine has to work <u>much harder</u> just to maintain a <u>steady speed</u>.
3) It therefore uses <u>more petrol</u> than it would going just as far at 30mph.

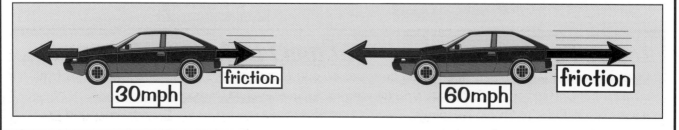
30mph   friction   60mph   friction

Friction

The Idea of Resultant Force is Real Important

1) The notion of _RESULTANT FORCE_ is a real important one for you to get your head round.
2) It's not especially tricky, it's just that it seems to get kind of _ignored_.
3) In most _real situations_ there are _at least two forces_ acting on an object along any direction.
4) For any _moving object_ there's always some sort of force _pushing_ the thing and then there's always the _good old dependable DRAG_ (or air resistance) trying to _slow the thing down_.

5) The _overall effect_ of these forces will decide the _motion_ of the object — whether it will _accelerate_, _decelerate_ or stay at a _steady speed_.

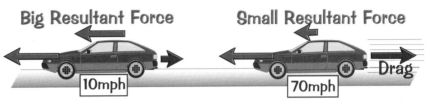
Big Resultant Force   Small Resultant Force   Drag
10mph   70mph

6) The _"overall effect"_ is found by just _adding or subtracting_ the forces which point along the _same_ direction. The overall force you get is called the _RESULTANT FORCE_.

But We Also Need Friction to Move and to Stop!

1) It's easy to think of friction as generally a _nuisance_ because we always seem to be working _against it_.
2) But don't forget that _without it_ we wouldn't be able to _walk_ or _run_ or _race off the line at the traffic lights_ or _screech round corners_ or go _sky-diving_ or do just about anything exciting or interesting.
3) It also holds _nuts and bolts_ together.
4) Life _without_ friction — that _would_ be a drag.

Friction Causes Wear and Heating

1) Friction always acts _between surfaces_ that are _sliding over_ each other. _Machinery_ has lots of surfaces doing that.
2) Friction always produces _heat_ and _wearing_ of the surfaces.
3) _Lubricants_ are used to keep the friction as _low_ as possible.

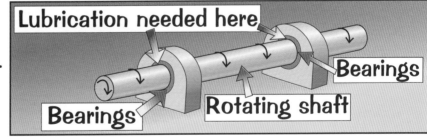
Lubrication needed here
Bearings
Rotating shaft
Bearings

4) This makes the machinery run more _freely_ so it needs _less power_, and it also _reduces wear_.
5) The _heating effect_ of friction can be _enormous_. For example the _brakes_ on _grand prix racing cars_ can often _glow red hot_.
6) Another example is if an engine is run _without oil_ it will quickly _seize up_ as the moving parts get _red hot_ through friction and eventually _weld_ themselves together.

Learn about friction — just don't let it wear you down...

I would never have thought there was so much to say about friction. Nevertheless, there it all is, all mentioned in the syllabuses, and all very likely to come up in your Exam. Ignore it at your peril. _Learn_ the eight main headings, then the stuff — then _cover the page_ and away you go.

The Three Laws of Motion

Around about the time of the Great Plague in the 1660s, a chap called _Isaac Newton_ worked out _The Three Laws of Motion_. At first they might seem kind of obscure or irrelevant, but to be perfectly blunt, if you can't understand these _three simple laws_ then you'll never fully understand _forces and motion_:

First Law — Balanced Forces mean No Change in Velocity

So long as the forces on an object are all _BALANCED_, then it'll just _STAY STILL_, or else if it's already moving it'll just carry on at the _SAME VELOCITY_ — so long as the forces are all _BALANCED_.

1) When a train or car or bus or anything else is _moving_ at a _constant velocity_ then the _forces_ on it must all be _BALANCED_.

2) Never allow yourself to entertain the _ridiculous idea_ that things need a constant overall force to _keep_ them moving — NO NO NO NO NO NO!

3) To keep going at a _steady speed_, there must be _ZERO RESULTANT FORCE_ — and don't you forget it.

Second Law — A Resultant Force means Acceleration

If there is an _UNBALANCED FORCE_, then the object will _ACCELERATE_ in that direction. The size of the acceleration is decided by the formula: F = ma.

1) An _unbalanced force_ will always produce _acceleration_ (or deceleration).

2) This "_acceleration_" can take _FIVE_ different forms:
Starting, _stopping_, _speeding up_, _slowing down_ and _changing direction_.

3) On a _force diagram_, the _arrows_ will be _unequal_:

Don't ever say: "If something's moving there must be an overall resultant force acting on it". Not so. If there's an _overall force_ it will always _accelerate_. You get _steady speed_ from _balanced_ forces. I wonder _how many times_ I need to say that _same thing_ before you _remember it_?

The Overall Unbalanced Force is often called The Resultant Force

Any _resultant force_ will produce _acceleration_.
The _size of the acceleration_ depends on how big the _resultant force_ is compared to the _mass_:

Three Points Which Should Be Obvious:

1) The bigger the _force_, the _GREATER_ the _acceleration_ or _deceleration_.

2) The bigger the _mass_ the _SMALLER the acceleration_.

3) To get a _big mass_ to accelerate _as fast_ as a _small mass_ it needs a _bigger force_.
Just think about pushing _heavy trolleys_ and it should all seem _fairly obvious_, I would hope.

The Three Laws of Motion

The Third Law — Reaction Forces

If object A _EXERTS A FORCE_ on object B then object B exerts _THE EXACT OPPOSITE FORCE_ on object A.

1) That means if you _push against a wall_, the wall will _push back_ against you, _just as hard_.
2) And as soon as you _stop_ pushing, _so does the wall_. Kinda clever really.
3) If you think about it, there must be an _opposing force_ when you lean against a wall — otherwise you (and the wall) would _fall over_.

4) If you _pull a cart_, whatever force _you exert_ on the rope, the rope exerts the _exact opposite_ pull on _you_.

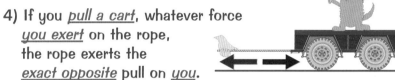

5) If you put a book on a table, the _weight_ of the book acts _downwards_ on the table — and the table exerts an _equal and opposite_ force _upwards_ on the book.

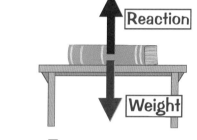

6) If you support a book on your _hand_, the book exerts its _weight_ downwards on you, and you provide an _upwards_ force on the book and it all stays _nicely in balance_.

Learn About Those Reaction Force Arrows

In _Exam questions_ they may well _test this_ by getting you to fill in some _extra arrow_ to represent the _reaction force_. Learn this _very important fact_:

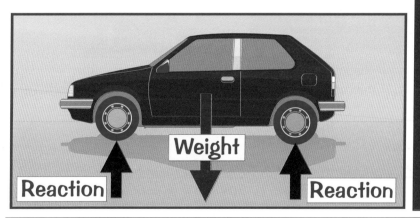

Whenever an object is on a horizontal _SURFACE_, there'll always be a _REACTION FORCE_ pushing _UPWARDS_, supporting the object. The total _REACTION FORCE_ will be _EQUAL AND OPPOSITE_ to the weight.

Hey, did you know — an unbalanced force causes ac...

Good old Isaac. Those three laws of motion are pretty inspirational don't you think? No? Oh. Well you could do with learning them anyway, because in this topic there are hardly any nice easy facts that'll help — in the end there's _no substitute_ for fully understanding _The Three Laws_.

Speed, Velocity and Acceleration

Speed and Velocity are Both just: HOW FAST YOU'RE GOING

Speed and velocity are both measured in *m/s* (or km/h or mph). They both simply say *how fast* you're going, but there's *a subtle difference* between them which *you need to know*:

SPEED is just **HOW FAST** you're going (e.g. 30 mph or 20 m/s) with no regard to the direction. **VELOCITY** however must **ALSO** have the **DIRECTION** specified, e.g. 30 mph *north* or 20 m/s, 060°

Seems kinda fussy I know, but they expect you to remember that distinction, so there you go.

Speed, Distance and Time — the Formula:

$$Speed = \frac{Distance}{Time}$$

You really ought to get *pretty slick* with this *very easy formula*.
As usual the *formula triangle* version makes it all a bit of a *breeze*.
You just need to try and think up some interesting word for remembering *the order of the letters* in the triangle, s^{d}t. Errm... sedit, perhaps... well, you think up your own.

EXAMPLE: *A cat skulks 20m in 35s. Find a) its speed b) how long it takes to skulk 75m.*
ANSWER: Using the formula triangle: a) s = d/t = 20/35 = <u>0.57 m/s</u>
b) t = d/s = 75/0.57 = 131s = <u>2mins 11sec</u>

A lot of the time we tend to use the words "speed" and "velocity" interchangeably.
For example to calculate velocity you'd just use the above formula for speed instead.

Acceleration is How Quickly You're Speeding Up

Acceleration is <u>DEFINITELY NOT</u> the same as *velocity* or *speed*.
Every time you read or write the word *acceleration*, remind yourself: "*acceleration is COMPLETELY DIFFERENT from velocity*. Acceleration is *how quickly* the velocity is *changing*."
Velocity is a simple idea. Acceleration is altogether more *subtle*, which is why it's *confusing*.

Acceleration — The Formula:

$$Acceleration = \frac{Change\ in\ Velocity}{Time\ Taken}$$

Well, it's *just another formula*. Just like all the others. Three things in a *formula triangle*. Mind you, there are *two tricky things* with this one. First there's the "ΔV", which means working out the "*change in velocity*", as shown in the example below, rather than just putting a *simple value* for speed or velocity in. Secondly there's the *units* of acceleration which are m/s². *Not m/s*, which is *velocity*, but m/s². Got it? No? Let's try once more: *Not m/s, but m/s².*

EXAMPLE: *A skulking cat accelerates from 2m/s to 6m/s in 5.6s. Find its acceleration.*
ANSWER: Using the formula triangle: a = ΔV/t = (6 - 2) / 5.6 = 4 ÷ 5.6 = <u>0.71 m/s²</u>
All pretty basic stuff I'd say.

Velocity and Acceleration — learn the difference...

It's true — some people don't realise that velocity and acceleration are totally different things. Hard to believe I know — all part of the great mystery and tragedy of life I suppose. Anyway. Learn the definitions and the formulae, *cover the page* and *scribble it all down again*.

Distance-Time and Velocity-Time Graphs

Make sure you learn all these details real good. Make sure you can _distinguish_ between the two, too.

Distance-Time Graphs

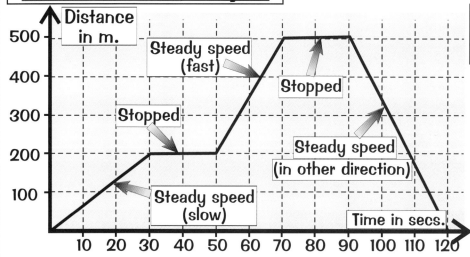

Four Very Important Notes:

1) _Flat sections_ are where it's _stopped_.
2) The _steeper_ the graph, the _faster_ it's going.
3) _Uphill_ sections (⟋) mean it's _travelling away_ from its starting point.
4) _Downhill_ sections (⟍) mean it's _coming back_ toward its starting point.

Calculating Speed from a Distance-Time Graph

For example the _speed_ of the _return section_ of the graph is:

$$\text{Speed} = \frac{\text{distance travelled}}{\text{time taken}} = \frac{500}{30} = \underline{16.7 \text{ m/s}}$$

Velocity-Time Graphs

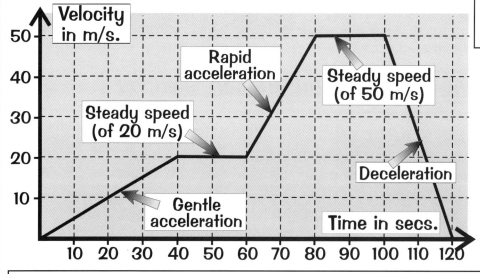

Four Very Important Notes:

1) _Flat sections_ represent _steady speed_.
2) The _steeper_ the graph, the _greater_ the _acceleration_ or _deceleration_.
3) _Uphill_ sections (⟋) are _acceleration_.
4) _Downhill_ sections (⟍) are _deceleration_.

Calculating Acceleration and Speed from a Velocity-time Graph

1) The _ACCELERATION_ represented by the _first section_ of the graph is:

$$\text{Acceleration} = \frac{\text{change in speed}}{\text{time interval}} = \frac{20}{40} = \underline{0.5 \text{ m/s}^2}$$

2) The _SPEED_ at any point is simply found by _reading the value_ off the _speed axis_.

Understanding speed and stuff — it can be an uphill struggle...

The tricky thing about these two kinds of graph is that they can look pretty much the same but represent totally different kinds of motion. If you want to be able to do them (in the Exam) then there's no substitute for simply _learning all the numbered points_ for both types. Enjoy.

Air Resistance and Terminal Velocity

Cars and Free-Fallers all Reach a Terminal Velocity

1) When either cars or free-falling objects _first set off_ they have _much more_ force _accelerating_ them than _resistance_ slowing them down.

2) As the _speed_ increases the resistance _builds up_.

3) This gradually _reduces_ the _acceleration_ until eventually the _resistance force_ is _equal_ to the _accelerating force_ and then it won't be able to accelerate any more.

4) It will have reached its maximum speed or _TERMINAL VELOCITY_.

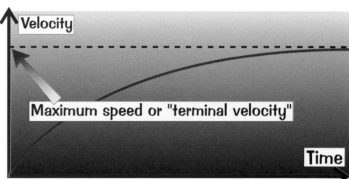

The Terminal Velocity of Falling Objects depends on their Shape and Area

1) The _accelerating force_ acting on _all falling objects_ is _GRAVITY_ and it would make them all fall at the _same rate_, if it wasn't for _air resistance_.

2) To prove this, _on the moon_, where there's _no air_, hamsters and feathers dropped simultaneously will _hit the ground together_.

3) However, on Earth, _air resistance_ causes things to fall at _different speeds_, and the _terminal velocity_ of any object is determined by its _drag_ in _comparison_ to the _weight_ of it. The _drag_ depends on its _shape and area_.

The Most Important Example is the Human Skydiver

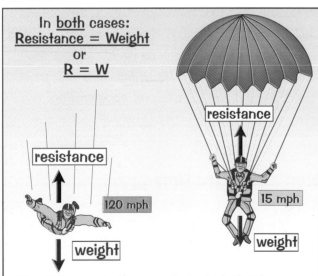

In _both_ cases:
Resistance = Weight
or
R = W

resistance

resistance

120 mph

15 mph

weight

weight

The difference is the _speed_ at which that happens

1) Without his parachute open he has quite a _small area_ and a force of "_W=mg_" pulling him down. He reaches a _terminal velocity_ of about _120 mph_.

2) But with the parachute _open_, there's much more _air resistance_ (at any given speed) and still only the same force "_W=mg_" pulling him down. For a while there's a much bigger drag force, which _slows him right down_.

3) Because of the _extra drag_ of the _open parachute_, his _terminal velocity_ comes right down to about _15 mph_, which is a _safe speed_ to hit the ground at.

Learning about Air resistance — it can be a real drag...

It looks like mini-essay time to me. There's a lot of details swirling around here, so definitely the best way of checking how much you know is to _scribble down a mini-essay_ for each of the three sections. Then _check back_ and see what you _missed_. Then try again. _And keep trying_.

Stopping Distances For Cars

They're pretty keen on this for Exam questions, so make sure you _learn it properly_.
The distance it takes to stop a car is divided into _THINKING DISTANCE_ and _BRAKING DISTANCE_.

1) Thinking Distance

"The distance the car travels in the split-second between a hazard appearing and the driver applying the brakes".

The thinking distance is affected by _THREE MAIN FACTORS_:

a) _How FAST you're going_ — obviously. Whatever your reaction time, the _faster_ you're going, the _further_ you'll go.

b) _How DOPEY you are_ — This is affected by _tiredness_, _drugs_, _alcohol_, _old-age_, and a _careless_ blasé attitude.

c) _How BAD the VISIBILITY is_ — lashing rain and oncoming lights, etc. make _hazards_ harder to spot.

2) Braking Distance

"The distance the car travels during its deceleration whilst the brakes are being applied."

The braking distance is affected by _FOUR MAIN FACTORS_:

a) _How FAST you're going_ — obviously. The _faster_ you're going the _further_ it takes to stop (see below).

b) _How HEAVILY LOADED the vehicle is_ — with the _same_ brakes, a _heavily-laden_ vehicle takes _longer to stop_. A car won't stop as quick when it's full of people and luggage and towing a caravan.

c) _How good your BRAKES are_ — all brakes must be _checked and maintained regularly_. Worn or faulty brakes will let you down _catastrophically_ just when you need them the _most_, i.e. in an _emergency_.

d) _How good the GRIP is_ — this depends on _THREE THINGS_:
1) _road surface_, 2) _weather_ conditions, 3) _tyres_.

1) Leaves and diesel spills and muck on t'road are _serious hazards_ because they're _unexpected_.
2) _Wet_ or _icy roads_ are always _much more slippy_ than dry roads, but often you only discover this when you try to _brake_ hard! Tyres should have a minimum _tread depth_ of _1.6mm_.
3) This is essential for _getting rid of the water_ in wet conditions. _Without tread_, a tyre will simply _ride_ on a _layer of water_ and skid _very easily_. This is called "_aquaplaning_" and isn't nearly as cool as it sounds.

Stopping Distances Increase Alarmingly with Extra Speed

To stop a car, the _kinetic energy_, has to be _converted to heat energy_ at the _brakes and tyres_:

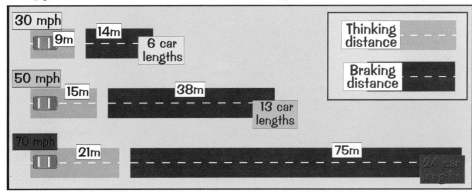

The figures shown here for _typical stopping distances_ are from the _Highway Code_. It's frightening to see _just how far it takes_ to _STOP_ when you're going at 70 mph.

30 mph — 9m — 14m — 6 car lengths
50 mph — 15m — 38m — 13 car lengths
70 mph — 21m — 75m — 24 car lengths

Thinking distance
Braking distance

Muck on t'road, eh — by gum, it's grim up North...

They mention this specifically in the syllabus and are very likely to test you on it since it involves safety. Learn all the details and write yourself a _mini-essay_ to see how much you _really know_.

Hooke's Law

Hooke's Law — Extension is Proportional to Load

Hooke's Law is _seriously easy_. It just says:

> If you **STRETCH** something with a **STEADILY INCREASING FORCE**, then the **LENGTH** will **INCREASE STEADILY** too.

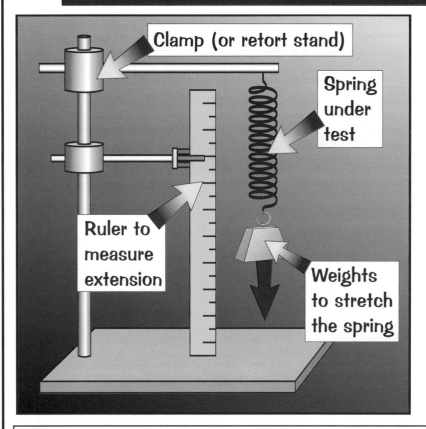

1) The important thing to measure in a Hooke's Law experiment is not so much the total length as the _EXTENSION_:

> **EXTENSION** is the **INCREASE IN LENGTH** compared to the _original length_ with _no force applied_.

2) For most materials, you'll find that _THE EXTENSION IS PROPORTIONAL TO THE LOAD_.
3) This just means that if you _double_ the load, the _extension is double too_.

Hooke's Law is Only The Straight Bit of These Graphs

When the extension _is_ proportional to the load it gives _a straight line graph through the origin_. Learn these _THREE IMPORTANT CASES_: a _METAL WIRE_, a _SPRING_ and a _RUBBER BAND_.

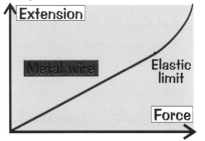
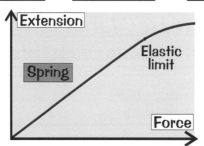
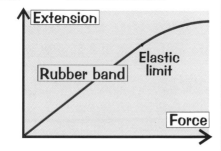

1) Notice that _in all three cases_ there's an _elastic limit_.
2) For extensions _less_ than this, the wire or spring _returns to its original shape_.
3) But if the thing is stretched _beyond_ the elastic limit, it behaves _inelastically_.
4) This means it _doesn't_ follow Hooke's law and that it also _won't return_ to its original shape.

Hooke's Law — it can stretch you to the limit...

Hooke's Law is pretty standard stuff really, so make sure you know all those little details, including the graphs, and the reasons behind their straight bits and their curved bits. Then find out what you know: _Cover the page, scribble down what you know, check it, try again, etc._

Forces Acting on Solids

Stretching, Compressing, Bending, Twisting, Shearing...

When a *combination of forces* are applied to a *solid object*, they can cause *different effects*:

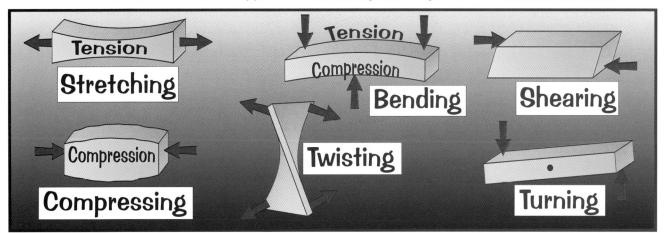

1) Make sure you can put in *all the forces* in all the *right places* and also identify in each case where/whether the solid is under *tension* or *compression*.
2) Note that sometimes an object does *not return* to its *original shape* when the forces are removed.
3) This is known as *INELASTIC BEHAVIOUR*. (See Hooke's Law on the previous page.)

Moments are Turning Forces

When a force acts on something which has a *pivot*, it creates a *turning force* called a *"moment"*.

MOMENTS are *calculated* using this formula:

MOMENT = force × perpendicular distance

M = F × r

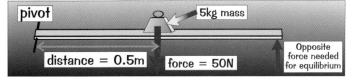

In this example, the *moment* due to the *5kg mass* is:

"Moment = F×r" = 50N × 0.5m = **25 Nm**

Also, for the system to be in *equilibrium*, (i.e. all *nicely balanced* and *not moving*) then:

total *clockwise* moment = total *anticlockwise* moment

In the above example, the *balancing force* (pointing upwards) must provide a *moment* of *25 Nm anticlockwise* to balance the *clockwise moment* due to the 5kg mass. If the balancing force is *twice as far away* it will only need to be *half as big*, i.e. *25N*, compared to the weight of 50N.

What's a turning force called? — just a moment...

Make sure you can do all those diagrams on pummelling solids. Also make sure you know what a moment is, and the formula for calculating moments. When you know it all, *cover the page* and *scribble it down*, including the example on moments. Then *see how you did*, and *try again*.

Pressure on Surfaces

Too many people get *force* and *pressure* mixed up — but there's a *pretty serious difference* between them. It's a bit *subtle* though so you have to *concentrate quite hard* to get it. Read on, learn, and squirm with pleasure as another great mystery of the Physical Universe is exposed to your numb and weary mind...

Pressure is Defined As the Force Acting on Unit Area of a Surface

$$\text{Pressure} = \frac{\text{Force}}{\text{Area}}$$

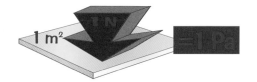

The normal *unit of pressure* is the *Pascal*, Pa, which is the same as N/m^2.

Watch out for Areas in cm²

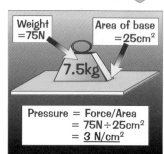

Pressure = Force/Area
= 75N ÷ 25cm²
= 3 N/cm²

1) They may well give you questions with areas given in *cm²*.
2) Don't try to *convert cm² to m²* which is a bit tricky.
3) Instead, just work out the pressure using P = F/A in the normal way, but give the answer as N/cm^2 rather than N/m^2 (Pa).
4) Do remember that *N/cm²* is *not* the same as Pascals (which are N/m^2).

Force vs Pressure has a lot to do with Damaging Surfaces

1) A force concentrated in a *small area* creates a *high pressure*.
2) That means the thing will *sink into the surface*.
3) But with a *big area*, you get a *low pressure* which spreads the load out.
4) That means it *doesn't* sink into the surface. *Learn* these examples:

A Force Spread over a Big Area means Low Pressure and No Sinking

Foundations   Snow shoes   Tractor tyres   Drawing pins

A Force Concentrated on a Small Area means High Pressure and Damage

Ice skates   Stiletto heels   Sharp knives   Drawing pins

Spread the load and reduce the pressure — start revising now...

It's funny old stuff is pressure. Force is a nice easy concept and people usually do fine with it. But pressure is just that bit trickier — and that means it can cause people a lot of gip. Make sure you *learn all these details* about pressure. They're all worth marks in the Exam.

Pressure = Force/Area

Hydraulics — the Main Application of "P = F/A"

Hydraulic systems all use _two important features_ of _pressure in liquids_. _LEARN THEM_:

> 1) __PRESSURE IS _TRANSMITTED THROUGHOUT THE LIQUID___, so that the force can easily be applied _WHEREVER YOU WANT IT_, using flexible pipes.
>
> 2) The force can be _MULTIPLIED_ according to the _AREAS_ of the pistons used.

Small Master Cylinder Area...

1) All hydraulic systems use a _SMALL master piston_ and a _BIG slave piston_.
2) The _master piston_ is used to _apply a force_ which puts the liquid _under pressure_.
3) This pressure is _transmitted_ throughout _all the liquid_ in the system, and somewhere _at the other end_ it pushes on the _slave piston_ which _exerts a force_ where it's needed.

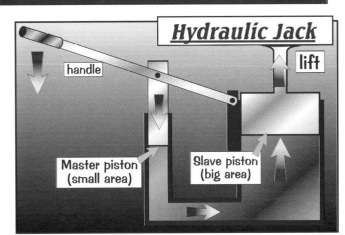

Hydraulic Jack

handle — lift — Master piston (small area) — Slave piston (big area)

...Big Slave Cylinder Area

4) The _slave piston_ always has a _much larger area_ than the _master piston_ so that it exerts a _much greater force_ from the pressure created by the force on the master piston. Clever stuff.
5) In this way, _hydraulic systems_ are used as _force multipliers_, i.e. they use a _small force_ to create a _very big force_ — a nice trick if you can do it.

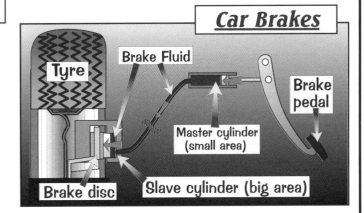

Car Brakes

Tyre — Brake Fluid — Brake pedal — Master cylinder (small area) — Slave cylinder (big area) — Brake disc

The Typical Method for the Typical Exam Question:

1) Use the _master cylinder area_ and _force_ to calculate _the pressure in the system_,   P = F/A
2) Apply this pressure to the _area of the slave piston_ to calculate the _force exerted_,   F = P×A

EXAMPLE: The car master piston has an area of 4cm². If a force of 400N is applied to it, calculate the pressure created in the brake pipes. If the slave piston has an area of 40cm² calculate the force exerted on the brake disc.
ANSWER: The usual _two step method_:

1) At the _master piston_: Pressure created = F/A = 400N÷4cm² = __100 N/cm²__ (Not Pascals!)

2) At the _slave piston_: Force produced = P×A = 100×40 = __4000N__ (10 times original force)

Learn about hydraulics — and make light work of it...

You certainly need to know that formula for pressure, but that's pretty easy. The really tricky bit which you need to concentrate most on is how that formula is applied (twice) to explain how hydraulic systems turn a small force into a big one. _Keep working at it till you understand it._

Pressure in Liquids

Pressure in Liquids Acts in All Directions and Increases With Depth

1) In a _gas_ or _liquid_ the same pressure acts _outwards in all directions_.
2) This is _different from solids_ which transmit forces in _one direction only_.
3) Also, the _pressure_ in a liquid or gas _increases_ as you go _deeper_.
4) This is due to the _weight_ of all the stuff _above it_ pushing down. Imagine the weight of all the water _directly over you_ at a depth of 100m.
5) All of that is _pushing down_ on the water below and _increasing the pressure_ down there.
6) This is what _limits the depth_ that submarines can go to before the pressure _crushes the hull_ or bursts through a _weak join_ somewhere.

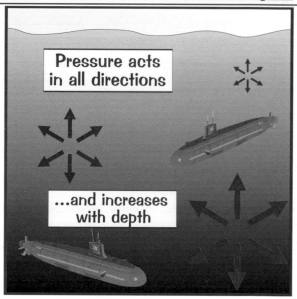

Pressure acts in all directions

...and increases with depth

The Increase in Pressure With Depth Depends on Density Too

1) The _increase in pressure_ also depends on the _density_ of the fluid.
2) Air is _not very dense_, so air pressure changes _relatively little_ as you go up through the atmosphere. It changes from zero at the top of the atmosphere to a pressure of just one atmosphere at ground level.
3) Water _is pretty dense_ though, so the pressure increases very quickly as you go _deeper_. You only have to go down _10 metres under water_ for the pressure to become _double_ normal atmospheric pressure.

Dams are Made Wedge-Shaped due to the Increasing Pressure

1) They mention this _specifically_ in the syllabus as the classic consequence of how the _pressure increases with depth_ in a fluid, so _make sure_ you learn it.
2) _Dams_ have to be made _much thicker_ at the _bottom_ to cope with the _massive pressures_ which are created by the _weight of water_ above.

3) Note the figures for 50m and 100m. Those are _real big pressures_, and when acting on the _large area_ of a dam they create _monster forces_. Ideal for disaster movies.

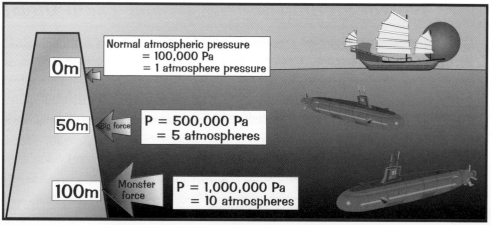

0m — Normal atmospheric pressure = 100,000 Pa = 1 atmosphere pressure
50m — Big force — P = 500,000 Pa = 5 atmospheres
100m — Monster force — P = 1,000,000 Pa = 10 atmospheres

Learn about pressure — in great depth...

This is a nice easy page to finish off Section Two, don't you think? There's only about two main things to learn on the whole page. But you could easily get a nice friendly Exam Question giving away oodles of easy marks asking why dams are thicker at the bottom. _Grab those easy ones._

Revision Summary for Section Two

More jolly questions which I know you're going to really enjoy. There are lots of bits and bobs on forces, motion and pressure which you definitely need to know. Some bits are certainly quite tricky to understand, but there's also loads of straightforward stuff which just needs to be learnt, ready for instant regurgitation in the Exam. You have to practise these questions over and over and over again, until you can answer them all really easily — phew, such jolly fun.

1) What is gravity? List the three main effects that gravity produces.
2) Explain the difference between mass and weight. What units are they measured in?
3) What's the formula for weight? Illustrate it with a worked example of your own.
4) List the six different kinds of force. Sketch diagrams to illustrate them all.
5) Sketch each of the five standard force diagrams, showing the forces and the type of motion.
6) List the three types of friction with a sketch to illustrate each one.
7) Describe how friction is affected by speed.
8) Explain what "resultant force" is. Illustrate it with a diagram.
9) What two effects does friction have on machinery?
10) Is friction at all useful? Describe five problems we would have if there was no friction.
11) Write down the First Law of Motion. Illustrate it with a diagram.
12) Write down the Second Law of Motion. Illustrate it with a diagram.
13) Write down the Third Law of Motion. Illustrate it with four diagrams.
14) Explain what *reaction force* is and where it pops up. Is it important to know about it?
15) What's the difference between speed and velocity? Give an example of each.
16) Write down the formula for working out speed.
17) Find the speed of a partly chewed mouse which hobbles 3.2m in 35s.
18) Find how far he would get in 25 minutes.
19) What is acceleration? Is it the same thing as speed or velocity? What are the units of it?
20) Write down the formula for acceleration.
21) What's the acceleration of a soggy pea, flicked from rest to a speed of 14 m/s in 0.4s?
22) What's the acceleration of a big fast car, powering from rest to a speed of 27 m/s in 6.1s?
23) Sketch a typical distance-time graph and point out all the important parts of it.
24) Sketch a typical velocity-time graph and point out all the important parts of it.
25) Write down four important points relating to each of these graphs.
26) Explain how to calculate velocity from a distance-time graph.
27) Explain how to find speed and acceleration from a velocity-time graph.
28) What is "terminal velocity"? Is it the same thing as maximum speed?
29) What are the two main factors affecting the terminal velocity of a falling object?
30) What are the two different parts of the overall stopping distance of a car?
31) List the factors which affect a) thinking distance and b) braking distance.
32) What happens to overall stopping distances as the speed increases?
33) What is Hooke's Law? Sketch the usual apparatus. Explain what you must measure.
34) Sketch the three Hooke's Law graphs and explain their shape. Explain "elastic" and "inelastic".
35) Sketch a solid undergoing: stretching; compressing; bending; twisting; shearing; turning.
36) What is a "moment"? What is the formula for moment? Illustrate it with a diagram.
37) What's the definition of pressure? What combination of force and area gives high pressure?
38) What's the formula for pressure? What units is pressure normally given in?
39) Sketch four diagrams showing how pressure is a) reduced and b) increased.
40) Write down the two features of pressure in liquids which allow hydraulic systems to work.
41) Sketch a jack and a car braking system and explain how they work as force multipliers.
42) What happens to pressure as you go deeper? Which direction does the pressure act in?

SECTION TWO — FORCES AND MOTION

Waves — Basic Features

Waves are different from anything else. They have various features which *only waves have*:

Amplitude, Wavelength and Frequency

Too many people get these *wrong*. Take careful note:

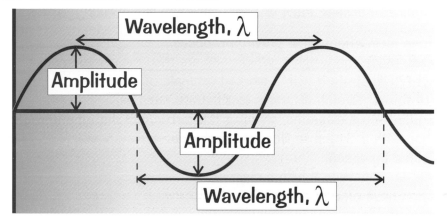

Don't be scared off by the *funny symbol*, "λ", will you.

λ is just a *harmless Greek letter*, called "*lambda*" (*say it as "lamda"*).
Try it yourself, go on: "*L-A-M-D-A*".
There, you see — doesn't hurt at all, does it.

1) The **AMPLITUDE** goes from the *middle line* to the *peak*, NOT from a trough to a peak.
2) The **WAVELENGTH** covers *a full cycle* of the wave, e.g. from *peak to peak*, not just from "*two bits that are sort of separated a bit*".
3) **FREQUENCY** is how many *complete waves* there are *per second* (passing a certain point).

All Waves Carry Energy — Without Transferring Matter

There are lots of *good examples* which show that all sorts of waves *carry energy*. *Learn these*:
1) *Light*, *infrared* and *microwaves* all make things *warm up*.   *X-rays* and *gamma rays* can cause *ionisation* and *damage* to cells, which also shows that they *carry energy*.
2) *Loud sounds* make things *vibrate or move*.   Even the quietest sound moves your *ear drum*.
3) Waves on the sea can *toss big boats around* and can *generate electricity*.
4) Waves also transfer *information*, as well as energy, e.g. TV, radio, speech, fibre optics, etc.

All Waves can be Reflected and Refracted

They might test whether or not you realise these two things are *properties of waves*, so *learn them*. The two words are *confusingly similar* but you **MUST** learn the *difference* between them.

1) *REFLECTION* is when a wave "*bounces off*" a surface and sets off in a *completely different direction*.
Reflection of *light* is obvious, e.g. from any shiny surface like a *mirror*.
Sound also reflects — it's called an *echo*. Sound will only be reflected from *hard flat surfaces*.   Things like *carpets* and *curtains* act as *absorbing surfaces* which will *absorb* sounds rather than reflect them.

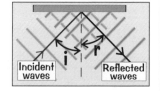

2) *REFRACTION* is when a wave *changes direction* as it *enters a different substance* (or "medium"). All waves refract (See P. 46).

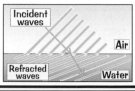

Learn about waves — just get into the vibes, man...

This is all pretty basic stuff on waves. *Learn* the headings, then all the details and diagrams. Then *cover the page* and see what you can *scribble down*. Then try again and again until you can remember the whole lot. It's all just *easy marks to be won... or lost*.

Transverse and Longitudinal Waves

Transverse Waves have Sideways Vibrations

Most waves are *TRANSVERSE*:

1) *Light* and *all other EM waves*.
2) *Ripples* on water.
3) *Waves* on *strings*.
4) A *slinky spring* wiggled *up and down*.

In *TRANSVERSE WAVES*
the vibrations are at *RIGHT ANGLES*
to the *direction of travel* of the wave.

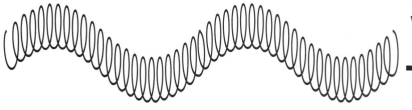

Vibrations from ↑side to side↑

Wave travelling this way →

Longitudinal Waves have Vibrations along the Same Line

The ONLY longitudinal waves are:

1) *Sound waves*.
2) *Shock waves*, e.g. from earthquakes.
3) A *slinky spring* when *plucked*.

In *LONGITUDINAL WAVES*
the vibrations are
ALONG THE SAME DIRECTION
as the wave is travelling.

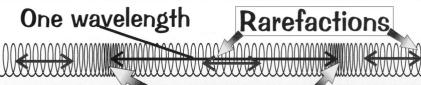

One wavelength

Rarefactions

Compressions

Vibrations in same direction

as wave is travelling

Microphones Turn Sound Waves into Electrical Signals

1) An electrical *"signal"* is simply a *varying electrical current*.
2) The *variations* in the current carry the *information*.
3) The currents from a *microphone* are *very small* and are amplified into *much bigger signals* by an amplifier.
4) These *signals* from the microphone can be *recorded* and played back through *speakers*.
5) Speakers turn *electrical signals* into *sound waves* — *exactly the opposite* of what a microphone does.
6) *Don't get confused* by CRO displays which show a *transverse wave* when displaying *sounds*. The real sound wave is *longitudinal* — the display shows a transverse wave *just so you can see what's going on*.

Transverse waves are like teenagers — all "ups" and "downs"...

People quite often have trouble remembering the difference between transverse and longitudinal waves. Well look, here it all is — all the juicy information you need, just waiting to be soaked up. *Learn* the headings, the diagrams and the details. Then *cover the page* and *scribble it down*.

Sound Waves

1) *Sound Waves Travel at Various Speeds in Different Substances*

1) *Sound Waves* are caused by *vibrating objects*.
2) Sound waves are *longitudinal waves*, which travel at *fixed speeds* in particular *media*, as shown in the table.
3) As you can see, the *denser* the medium, the *faster* sound travels through it, generally speaking anyway.
4) Sound generally travels *faster in solids* than in liquids, and faster in liquids than in gases.

Substance	Density	Speed of Sound
Iron	7.9 g/cm³	5000 m/s
Rubber	0.9 g/cm³	1600 m/s
Water	1.0 g/cm³	1400 m/s
Cork	0.3 g/cm³	500 m/s
Air	0.001 g/cm³	330 m/s

2) *Sound Doesn't Travel Through Vacuum*

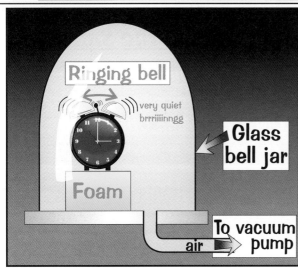

1) Sound waves can be *reflected* and *refracted*.
2) But one thing they *can't do* is travel through a *vacuum*.
3) This is *nicely demonstrated* by the jolly old *bell jar experiment*.
4) As the *air is sucked out* by the *vacuum pump*, the sound gets *quieter and quieter*.
5) The bell has to be *mounted* on something like *foam* to stop the sound from it travelling through the solid surface and making the *bench vibrate*, because you'd hear that *instead*.

3) *Noise Pollution — an Increasing Menace*

1) One source of *noise pollution* is *noisy machines* like *mowers*, *diggers* and *pneumatic drills*, etc.
2) Another is *noisy neighbours* with their ridiculous stereos, their barking dogs and their hooligan kids.
3) Noise pollution has many *harmful effects*, the main ones being *stress* and *distraction from work*.
4) Noise pollution can be *reduced* by:
   a) *SILENCING THE SOURCE*,
   b) *INSULATING HOMES*, *BUILDINGS* or just your *EARS*.

SPECIFIC WAYS OF REDUCING NOISE POLLUTION:

1) *FITTING SILENCERS* to *engines* and some sort of *MUFFLERS* to any other *machinery*.
2) *SOUND INSULATION* in *BUILDINGS*: *acoustic tiles*, *curtains*, *carpets* and *double glazing*.
3) And wearing *ear plugs*.

If sound travelled through vacuum — sunny days would be deafening...
Just to make your life easy, the page is broken up into sections with important numbered points for each. All those numbered points are important. They're all mentioned specifically in the syllabuses so you should expect them to test exactly this stuff in the Exams. *Learn and enjoy.*

Sound: Pitch and Loudness

The *pitch and loudness* of any sound are related to the wave *frequency and amplitude*. *Learn it*:

1) The Frequency of a Sound Wave Determines its Pitch

1) *High frequency sound waves* sound *HIGH PITCHED* like a *squeaking mouse*.
2) *Low frequency* sound waves sound *LOW PITCHED* like a *mooing cow*.
3) *Frequency* is the number of *complete vibrations* each second. It's measured in *Hertz, Hz*.
4) Other *common units* are *kHz* (1000Hz) and *MHz* (1,000,000Hz).
5) *High frequency* (or high pitch) also means *shorter wavelength*.
6) These *CRO screens* are *very important* so make sure you know all about them:

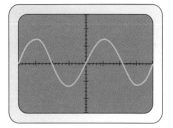
Original Sound

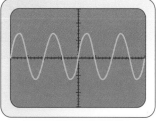
Higher pitched

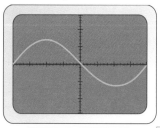
Lower pitched

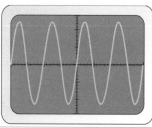
Higher pitched and louder

2) Amplitude is a Measure of the Energy Carried by Any Wave

1) The *greater the AMPLITUDE*, the *more ENERGY* the wave carries.
2) In *SOUND* this means it'll be *LOUDER*.
3) *Bigger amplitude* means *louder sound*.
4) With *LIGHT*, a bigger amplitude means it'll be *BRIGHTER*.

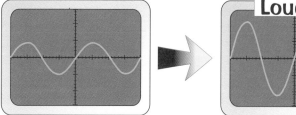
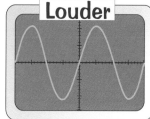
Louder

3) Your Hearing can be Damaged by Excessive Noise

1) The normal range of human hearing is *20Hz* to *20,000Hz*, but the upper limit *decreases with age*. Sounds with frequencies above 20,000Hz just *can't be heard*. Not by humans anyway.
2) *Dogs* however can hear up to about *40,000Hz* so dog whistles whistle between *20kHz* and *40kHz* so *we* can't hear them but the dogs *can*.
3) *Too much loud noise* will *damage* your hearing. The *higher end* of the frequency range is affected more. *Personal stereos* and *loud machinery* are the main culprits for wrecking people's hearing.

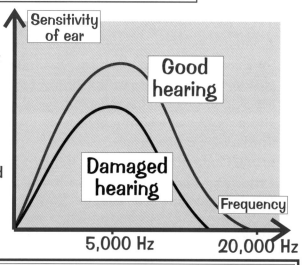

Amplitude? — isn't that a word to say how "chubby" you are...

Another page with three sections, etc. There does seem to be quite a lot of this stuff on boring ordinary waves and sound. But the simple truth is that the more of it you *really learn properly*, the more marks you'll get in the Exam. You do realise I hope that *most Exam questions*, even in Physics, simply test whether or not you've *learned the basic facts*. Just *easy marks* really.

Ultrasound

Ultrasound is simply sound with a higher frequency than we can hear — in other words sounds with frequencies higher than 20kHz. *ULTRASOUND* has loads of uses:

1) *Industrial Cleaning of Delicate Mechanisms and Teeth*

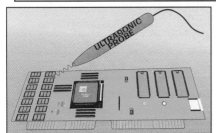

Ultrasound waves are extremely effective at *removing dirt* from *delicate equipment*.
The alternatives would either *damage* the equipment or else would require it to be *taken apart*.

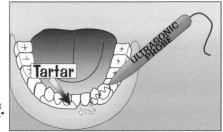

The same technique is used for *cleaning teeth*. Dentists use *ultrasonic tools* to easily and *painlessly* remove hard deposits of *tartar* which build up on teeth and can lead to *gum disease*.

2) *Industrial Quality Control*

Ultrasound waves can pass through a *metal casting* and when they reach a *crack or fault that shouldn't be there* then some of the wave is *reflected back* and *detected*. These *echoes* give *detailed information* about the *internal structure*.

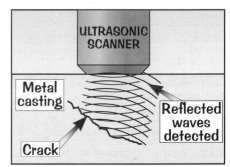

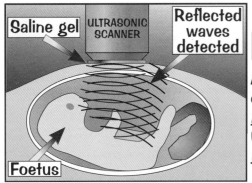

3) *For Pre-Natal Scanning of a Foetus*

As the ultrasound hits *different parts of the foetus* some of the ultrasound wave is *reflected* and this is *processed by computer* to produce a *video image* of the foetus. Ultrasound waves are *completely harmless* to the foetus, *unlike X-rays* which would be very dangerous.

4) *Range and Direction Finding — SONAR in Bats and Boats*

Bats send out *high-pitched squeaks* (ultrasound) and pick up the *reflections* with their *big ears*. Their brains are able to *process* the reflected signal and turn it into a *picture* of what's around.
So the bats basically "*see*" with *sound waves*, well enough in fact to *catch moths* in *mid-flight* in *complete darkness* — it's a nice trick if you can do it.
The same technique is used for *SONAR* which uses *sound waves* *underwater* to detect features on the seabed. The *pattern* of the reflections indicates the *depth* and basic features.

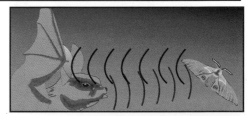

Ultrasound — weren't they a pop group...

Geesh — *another* page on sound, this time with *four* sections. No numbered points this time though. That means the mini-essay method is going to be a better idea this time. *Learn* the four headings, then *cover the page* and *scribble a mini-essay* for each, with diagrams. Enjoy.

Reflection: a Property of all Waves

The Ripple Tank is Really Good for Displaying Waves

Learn all of this diagram showing _reflection of water waves_.

They could ask you to complete _a similar one_ in the Exam.

It can be quite a bit _trickier_ than you think unless you've _practised_ it real well _beforehand_.

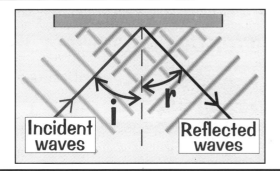

Reflection of Light

1) _Reflection of light_ is what allows us to _SEE_ objects.
2) When light reflects from an _uneven surface_ such as a _piece of paper_ the light reflects off _at all different angles_ and you get a _DIFFUSE REFLECTION_.
3) When light reflects from an _even surface_ (_smooth and shiny_ like a _mirror_) then it's all reflected at the _same angle_ and you get a _clear reflection_.
4) But don't forget, whether it reflects off an even surface or a rough one, _THE LAW OF REFLECTION_ applies to _every reflected ray_:

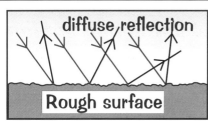
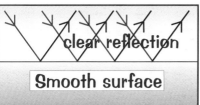

Angle of _INCIDENCE_ = Angle of _REFLECTION_

Reflection In a Plane Mirror — How to Locate The Image

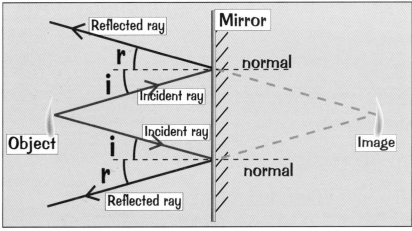

You need to be able to _reproduce_ this entire diagram of _how an image is formed_ in a _PLANE MIRROR_. Learn these _three important points_:

1) The _image_ is the _SAME SIZE_ as the _object_.
2) It is _AS FAR BEHIND_ the mirror as the object is _in front_.
3) It's formed from _diverging rays_, which means it's a _virtual image_.

1) _To draw any reflected ray_, just make sure the _angle of reflection_, r, equals the _angle of incidence_, i.
2) Note that these two angles are _ALWAYS_ defined between the ray itself and the _dotted NORMAL_.
3) _Don't ever_ label them as the angle between the ray and the _surface_. Definitely uncool.

Learn reflection thoroughly — try to look at it from all sides...

First make sure you can draw all those diagrams from memory. Then make sure you've learnt the rest well enough to answer typical meany Exam questions like these: _"Explain why you can see a piece of paper" "What is diffuse reflection?" "Why is the image in a plane mirror virtual?"_

Refraction: a Property of all Waves

1) *Refraction* is when waves *change direction* as they *enter a different substance (or "medium")*.
2) This is caused *entirely* by the *change in speed* of the waves.
3) It also causes the *wavelength* to change, but remember that the *frequency* does *not* change.

1) Refraction is Shown by Waves in a Ripple Tank Slowing Down

1) The waves travel *slower* in *shallower water*, causing *refraction* as shown.
2) There's a *change in direction*, and a *change in wavelength* but *NO change in frequency*.

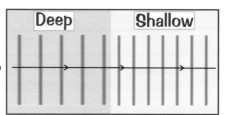

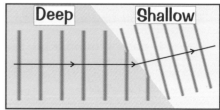

2) Refraction of Light — The Good Old Glass Block Demo

You can't fail to remember the old *"ray of light through a rectangular glass block"* trick.
Make sure you can draw this diagram *from memory*, with every detail *perfect*.

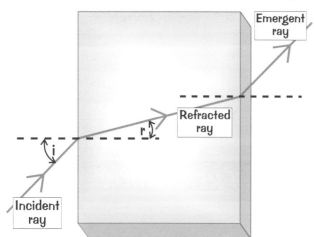

1) *Take careful note* of the positions of the *normals* and the *exact positions* of the angles of *incidence* and *refraction* (and note it's the angle of *refraction* — not reflection).
2) Most important of all remember *which way* the ray *bends*.
3) The ray bends *towards the normal* as it enters the *denser medium*, and *away* from the normal as it *emerges* into the *less dense* medium.
4) Try to *visualise* the shape of the *wiggle* in the diagram — that can be easier than remembering the rule in words.

3) Refraction Is always Caused By the Waves Changing Speed

1) When waves *slow down* they bend *towards* the normal.
2) When *light* enters *glass* it *slows down* to about *2/3 of its normal speed* (in air) i.e. it slows down to about 2×10^8 m/s rather than 3×10^8 m/s.
3) When waves hit the boundary *along a normal*, i.e. at *exactly 90°*, then there will be *no change* in direction. That's pretty important to remember, because they often *sneak it into a question* somewhere. There'll still be a change in *speed* and *wavelength*, though.
4) *Some* light is also *reflected* when light hits a *different medium* such as glass.

4) Sound Waves also Refract But it's Hard to Spot

Sound waves will also refract (change direction) as they enter *different media*. However, since sound waves are always *spreading out so much*, the change in direction is *hard to spot* under normal circumstances. But just remember, *sound waves do refract*, OK?

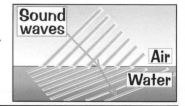

Revise Refraction — but don't let it slow you down...

The first thing you've gotta do is make sure you can spot the difference between the words *refraction* and *reflection*. After that you need to *learn all this stuff about refraction* — so you know exactly what it is. Make sure you know all those *diagrams* inside out. *Cover and scribble*.

Refraction: Two Special Cases

Dispersion Produces Rainbows

1) _Different colours of light_ are _refracted_ by _different amounts_.
2) This is because they travel at _slightly different speeds_ in any given _medium_.
3) A _prism_ can be used to make the different colours of white light emerge at _different angles_.

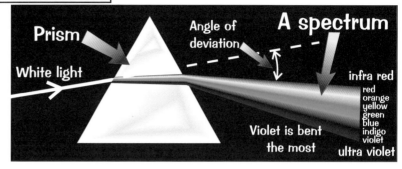

4) This produces a _spectrum_ showing all the colours of the _rainbow_. This effect is called _DISPERSION_.
5) You need to know that _red light_ is refracted the _least_ — and _violet_ is refracted the _most_.
6) Also know the _order of colours_ in between: Red Orange _____ Green Blue Indigo Violet
   which is remembered by: Richard Of ork ave Battle In Vain
   They may well test whether you can put them correctly into the diagram.
7) Also learn where _infrared_ and _ultraviolet_ light would appear if you could detect them.

Total Internal Reflection and The Critical Angle

1) This _only happens_ when _light_ is _coming out_ of something _dense_ like _glass_ or _water_ or _perspex_.
2) If the _angle_ is _shallow enough_ the ray _won't come out at all_, but it _reflects_ back into the glass (or whatever).   This is called _total internal reflection_ because _ALL_ of the light _reflects back in_.
3) You definitely need to learn this set of _THREE DIAGRAMS_ which show the three conditions:

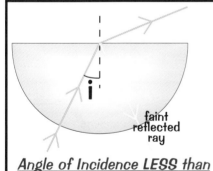

Angle of Incidence LESS than the Critical Angle.
Most of the light _passes through_ into the air but a _little_ bit of it is _internally reflected_.

Angle of Incidence EQUAL TO the Critical Angle.
The emerging ray comes out _along the surface_. There's quite a bit of _internal reflection_.

Angle of Incidence GREATER than the Critical Angle.
No light comes out. It's _all_ internally reflected, i.e. _total internal reflection_.

1) The _Critical Angle_ for _glass_ is about 42°. This is _very handy_ because it means _45° angle_s can be used to get _total internal reflection_ as in the _prisms_ in the _binoculars_ and _periscope_ shown on the next page.
2) In _DIAMOND_ the _Critical Angle_ is much _lower_, about _24°_. This is the reason why diamonds _sparkle_ so much, because there are lots of _internal reflections_.

Revision — sure it's Critical, but it's not a prism sentence...

First and foremost make sure you can _scribble all the diagrams_ down with all the details. Then _scribble a mini-essay_ for each topic, jotting down everything you can remember. Then check back and see what you _missed_. Then _learn the stuff you forgot_ and _try again_. Ahh... such fun.

Uses of Total Internal Reflection

Total Internal Reflection is used in *binoculars*, *periscopes* and *bicycle reflectors*. All three use *45° prisms*.

Binoculars

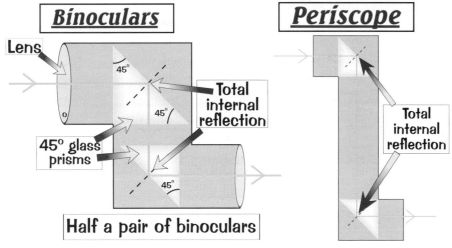

Half a pair of binoculars

Periscope

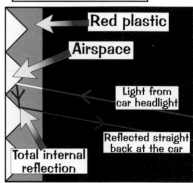

Reflectors

In the case of the *binoculars* and *periscope* the prisms give *slightly better reflection* than a *mirror* would and they're also *easier* to hold accurately *in place*. Learn the *exact positioning* of the prisms. They could ask you to *complete* a diagram of a binocular or periscope and unless you've *practised* beforehand you'll find it *pretty tricky* to draw the prisms in *properly*.

In the *bicycle reflectors* the prisms work cleverly by sending the light back in *exactly the opposite direction* that it came from (as shown in the diagram). This means that whoever *shines the light* gets a *strong reflection* straight back at their eyes.

Optical Fibres — Communications and Endoscopes

1) *Optical fibres* can carry *information* over *long distances* by repeated *total internal reflections*.
2) Optical communications have *several advantages* over *electrical signals* in wires:
   a) the signal doesn't need *boosting* as often,
   b) a cable of the *same diameter* can carry a lot *more information*,
   c) the signals cannot be *tapped into*, or suffer *interference* from electrical sources.
3) Normally no light whatever would be lost at each reflection. However *some light is lost* due to *imperfections* in the surface, so it still needs *boosting* every *few km*.

The fibre must be *narrow enough* to keep the angles *below the critical angle*, as shown, so the fibre mustn't be bent *too sharply* anywhere.

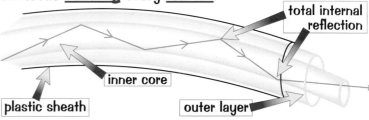

Endoscopes are Used to Look Inside People

This is a *narrow bunch* of *optical fibres* with a *lens system* at each end. Another bunch of optical fibres carries light down *inside* to see with.
The image is displayed as a *full colour moving image* on a **TV screen**. Real impressive stuff. This means they can do operations *without* cutting big holes in people. This was never possible before optical fibres.

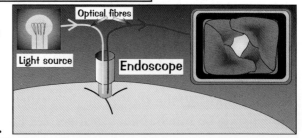

Total Internal Reflection — sounds like a Government Inquiry...

Three sections to learn here, with diagrams for each. They always have *at least one* of these applications of total internal reflection in the Exam. *Learn them all*. None of this is difficult — but just make sure you've got all those little picky details firmly fastened inside your head.

SECTION THREE — WAVES

Questions on The Speed of Sound

Relative Speeds of Sound and Light

1) _Light_ travels about _a million times faster_ than _sound_, so you never bother to calculate how long it takes compared to sound. You only work out the time taken for the _sound_ to travel.

2) The _formula_ needed is always the good old _s*d*t_ one for _speed, distance and time_ (see P. 30).

3) When something makes a sound more than about _100m away_ and you can actually _see_ the action which makes the sound then the effect is quite _noticeable_.   Good examples are:

a) _LIVE CRICKET_ — you hear the "_knock_" a while after seeing the ball being struck.

b) _HAMMERING_ — you hear the "_clang_" when the hammer is back up _in mid air_.

c) _STARTING PISTOL_ — you _see the smoke_ and then _hear the bang_.

d) _JET AIRCRAFT_ — they're always _ahead_ of where it sounds like they are.

e) _THUNDER AND LIGHTNING_ — the flash of lightning causes the sound of the thunder, and the _time interval_ between the _flash_ and the _rumble_ tells you how far away the lightning is. There's approximately _five seconds delay for every mile_.   (1 mile = 1600m,   ÷ 330 = 4.8s)

EXAMPLE: Looking out from his modest office across the Designated (EU Directive 672) Young Persons Recreation Area (i.e. the school yard), the Headmaster saw the five most troublesome and nauseating kids in his school destroying something nice with their horrid hammer.   Before acting swiftly, he did take the time to notice that there was a delay of exactly 0.4 seconds between the hammer striking and the sound reaching his shell-like ear.   So just how far away were these horrid children.   (Sound travels at 330m/s in air, as you know.)

ANSWER: The formula we want is of course "Speed = Distance/Time" or "s=d/t". We want to find the distance, d. We already know the time is 0.4s, and the speed of sound in air = 330m/s.   Hence d=s×t (from the triangle) This gives: d = 330×0.4 = _132m_.   (That's how far the sound travels in 0.4 secs.) Easy peasy.

Echo Questions — Don't Forget the Factor of Two

1) The _big thing_ to remember with _echo questions_ is that because the sound has to travel _both ways_, then to get the _right answer_ you'll need to either _double something_ or _halve something_.

2) Make sure you remember: sound travels at about _330 m/s in air_ and _1400 m/s in water_. Any echo question will likely be in air or water and if you have to work out the speed of the sound it's real useful to know what sort of number you should be getting. So for example, if you get 170 m/s for the speed of sound in air then you should realise you've _forgotten the factor of two_ somewhere, and then you can _easily go back and sort it_.

EXAMPLE: Having successfully expelled the five most troublesome and nauseating kids from his school, the jubilant Headmaster popped open a bottle of Champagne and heard the echo 0.6s later from the other side of his modest office. Just how big was this modest office?

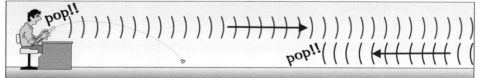

ANSWER: The formula is of course "Speed = Distance/Time" or "s=d/t". We want to find the distance, d. We already know the time, 0.6s, and the speed (of sound in air), hence d=s×t (from triangle). This gives: d = 330×0.6 = _198m_.   But Watch out! _Don't forget the factor of two for echo questions:_ The 0.6 secs is for _there and back_, so the office is only _half_ that distance, _99m long_.

Learn about Echos and the Factor of Two...Factor of Two...Factor of Two...

Learn the details on this page, then _cover it up_ and _scribble them down_. Then try these:

1) A man sees the cricketer hit the ball and hears the knock 0.6s later. How far away is he?

2) A ship sends a sonar signal to the sea bed and detects the echo 0.7s later. How deep is it?

The Electromagnetic Spectrum

There are Seven Basic Types of Electromagnetic Wave

The _properties_ of electromagnetic waves (EM waves) _change_ as the _frequency (or wavelength) changes_. There are _seven basic types_ as shown below.

RADIO WAVES	MICRO WAVES	INFRA RED	VISIBLE LIGHT	ULTRA VIOLET	X-RAYS	GAMMA RAYS
$1m-10^4 m$	$10^{-2} m$ (3cm)	$10^{-5} m$ (0.01mm)	$10^{-7} m$	$10^{-8} m$	$10^{-10} m$	$10^{-12} m$

Our _eyes_ can only detect a _narrow range_ of EM waves which are the ones we call (visible) _light_.
All EM waves travel at _exactly_ the same _speed_ as light in a _vacuum_.
In _other things_ (like glass or water) they still all travel at about the same speed as each other.

As the Wavelength Changes, So Do The Properties

1) As a rule the EM waves at _each end_ of the spectrum (e.g. radio waves or X-rays) _pass through materials_, whilst those _nearer the middle_ (e.g. visible light) are usually _absorbed by things_.

2) Also, the ones at the _top end_ (high frequency, short wavelength, like gamma rays) are the most _dangerous_, whilst those lower down (like radio waves) are _generally harmless_.

3) When _any electromagnetic radiation_ is _absorbed_ it can cause _two effects_:
   a) _Heating_.
   b) Creation of a _tiny alternating current_ with the _same frequency_ as the radiation.
      This is what happens in a radio receiver aerial when a radio or TV wave passes over it.

Radio Waves are Used Mainly For Communications

1) _Radio Waves_ are used mainly for _communication_ and, perhaps more importantly, for controlling model aeroplanes.

2) Both _TV and FM Radio_ use _short wavelength_ radio waves of about _1m wavelength_.

3) To receive these wavelengths you need to be more or less in _direct sight of the transmitter_, because they will _not_ bend over hills or travel very far _through_ buildings.

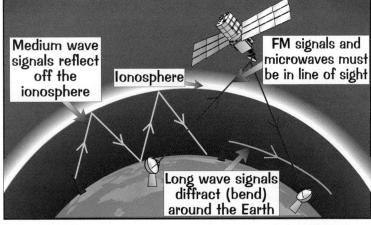

Medium wave signals reflect off the ionosphere

Ionosphere

FM signals and microwaves must be in line of sight

Long wave signals diffract (bend) around the Earth

4) _"Long Wave" radio_ on the other hand has wavelengths of about _1km_ and these waves _will_ bend over the surface of the Earth and also find their way into tunnels and all sorts.

5) _Medium Wave radio_ signals which have wavelengths of about _300m_ can be received _long distances_ from the transmitter because they are _reflected from the ionosphere_, which is an _electrically charged layer_ in the Earth's upper atmosphere. Mind you, these signals are always so fuzzy they're not worth listening to anyway (in my humble opinion).

The spectrum — isn't that something kinda rude in Biology...

There are lots of details on this page that you definitely need to know. The top diagram is an absolute must — they usually give it you with one or two missing labels to be filled in. _Learn_ the three sections on this page then _scribble_ a _mini-essay_ for each one to see what you know.

Microwaves and Infrared

Microwaves Are Used For Cooking and Satellite Signals

1) _Microwaves_ have _two main uses_: _cooking food_ and _satellite transmissions_.

2) These two applications use _two different frequencies_ of microwaves.

3) Satellite transmissions use a frequency which _passes easily_ through the _Earth's atmosphere_, including _clouds_, which seems pretty sensible.

4) The frequency used for _cooking_, on the other hand, is one which is _readily absorbed_ by _water molecules_. This is how a microwave oven works. The microwaves pass easily _into the food_ and are then _absorbed_ by the _water molecules_ and turn into heat _inside the food_.

5) Microwaves can therefore be _dangerous_ because they can be absorbed by _living tissue_ and the heat will _damage or kill the cells_ causing a sort of "_cold burn_".

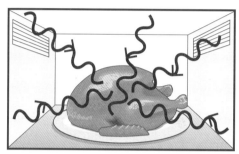

Infrared Radiation — Night-Vision and Remote Controls

1) _Infrared_ (or IR) is otherwise known as _heat radiation_. This is _given out_ by all _hot objects_ and you _feel it_ on your _skin_ as _radiant heat_. Infrared is readily _absorbed_ by _all materials_ and _causes heating_.

2) _Radiant heaters_ (i.e. those that _glow red_) use infrared radiation, including _toasters_ and _grills_.

3) _Over-exposure_ to infrared causes _damage to cells_. This is what causes _sunburn_. Note that it's the _infrared_ radiation which causes _sunburn_, but it's the _ultraviolet_ which causes _skin cancer_.

4) Infrared is also used for _night-vision equipment_. This works by detecting the _heat radiation_ given off by _all objects_, even in the dark of night, and turning it into an _electrical signal_ which is _displayed on a screen_ as a clear picture. The _hotter_ an object is, the _brighter_ it appears. _Police_ and the military use this to spot miscreants _running away_, like you've seen on TV.

5) Infrared is also used for all the _remote controls_ of _TVs and videos_. It's ideal for sending _harmless signals_ over _short distances_ without _interfering_ with other radio frequencies (like the TV channels).

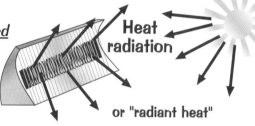

No escape from Infrared — if the Sun doesn't catch you, the Police will...

Each part of the EM spectrum is different, and you definitely need to know all the details about each type of radiation. These are just the kind of things they'll test in your Exams. Do _mini-essays_ for microwaves and IR. Then _check_ to see how you did. Then _try again... and again..._

Visible and UV Light, X-Rays and γ-Rays

Visible light is Used To See With and In Optical Fibres

Visible Light is pretty useful. We use it for seeing with for one thing. You could say (as one syllabus does!) that a use of it is in an _endoscope_ for seeing inside a patient's body, but let's face it, where do you draw the line? — it's also used in _microscopes_, _telescopes_, _kaleidoscopes_, pretend telescopes made of old toilet rolls, it's used for seeing in the dark (torch, lights, etc.), for saying "Hi" to people without speaking, and, perhaps most importantly, for controlling model aeroplanes. Seriously though, it's also used in _Optical Fibre Digital Communications_ which is the best one by far for your answer _in the Exam_.

Ultraviolet Light Causes Skin Cancer

1) This is what causes _skin cancer_ (and also possibly blindness) if you spend _too much time_ in the _sun_.
2) It also causes your skin to _tan_. _Sunbeds_ give out UV rays but _less harmful ones_ than the sun does.
3) _Darker skin_ protects against UV rays by _stopping_ them from reaching more _vulnerable skin tissues_ deeper down.
4) Ultraviolet is also useful for _hidden security marks_ which are written in special ink that can only be seen with an ultraviolet light.

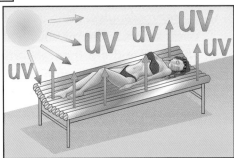

X-Rays Are Used in Hospitals, but are Pretty Dangerous

1) These are used in _hospitals_ to take _X-ray photographs_ of people to see whether they have any _broken bones_.
2) X-rays pass _easily through flesh_ but not through _denser material_ such as _bones_ or _metal_.
3) X-rays can cause _cancer_, so _radiographers_, who take X-ray pictures _all day long_ wear _lead aprons_ and stand behind a _lead screen_ to keep their _exposure_ to X-rays to a _minimum_.

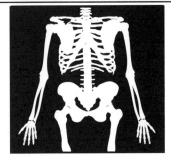

Gamma Rays Cause Cancer but Are Used to Treat it Too

1) Gamma rays are used to kill _harmful bacteria_ in food to keep it _fresher for longer_.
2) They are also used to _sterilise medical instruments_, again by _killing the bacteria_.
3) They can also be used in the _treatment of cancer_ because they _kill cancer cells_.
4) In _high doses_, gamma rays (along with X-rays and UV rays) can _kill normal cells_.
5) In _lower doses_ all these three types of EM waves can cause normal cells to become _cancerous_.

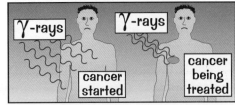

Radiographers are like Teachers — they can see right through you...

Here are the other four parts of the EM spectrum for you to learn. Ace, isn't it. At least there's some groovy diagrams to help relieve the tedium. On this page there are four sections.

Do a _mini-essay_ for each section, then _check_, _re-learn_, _re-scribble_, _re-check_, etc. etc.

Revision Summary for Section Three

One thing's for sure — there are loads of fairly easy facts to learn about waves. Of course there are still some bits which need thinking about, but really, most of it is fairly easy stuff which just needs learning. Don't forget, this book contains all the important information which they've specifically mentioned in the syllabus, and this is precisely the stuff they're going to test you on in the Exams. You must practise these questions over and over again until they're easy.

1) Sketch a wave and mark on it the amplitude and wavelength.
2) Define frequency for a wave. Give three examples of waves carrying energy.
3) Sketch a transverse wave. Give a definition for it.
4) Sketch a longitudinal wave. Give a definition for it.
5) Give four examples of transverse waves and two examples of longitudinal waves.
6) Explain what microphones and speakers do with sound waves and electrical signals.
7) Write down some typical speeds for sound in different materials.
8) Describe the bell jar experiment. What does it demonstrate?
9) Describe the menace of noise pollution.
10) What's the relationship between frequency and pitch for a sound wave?
11) What's the connection between amplitude and the energy carried by a wave?
12) What effect does greater amplitude have on   a) sound waves   b) light waves?
13) Sketch CRO screens showing higher and lower pitch and quiet and loud sounds.
14) Sketch graphs of normal and damaged hearing.   Give two causes of damaged hearing.
15) What is ultrasound? Give full details of four applications of ultrasound.
16) Sketch the pattern of reflected waves when plane ripples reflect at a plane surface.
17) Draw sketches to illustrate light reflecting from a rough surface and from an even surface.
18) What is a diffuse reflection? When do you get a diffuse reflection?
19) What is the law of reflection?
20) Draw a neat ray diagram to show how to locate the position of the image in a plane mirror.
21) What is refraction? What causes it? How does it affect wavelength and frequency?
22) Sketch water ripples moving into a shallower region   a) head on   b) at an angle.
23) Sketch a ray of light going through a rectangular glass block, showing the angles i and r.
24) How fast does light go in glass? Which way does it bend as it enters glass? What if i=90°?
25) What is dispersion. Sketch the diagram which illustrates it with all the labels.
26) Sketch the three diagrams to illustrate Total Internal Reflection and the Critical Angle.
27) Sketch three applications of total internal reflection which use 45° prisms, and explain them.
28) How do optical fibres work?
29) Give details of the two main uses of optical fibres.
30) How do the speeds of sound and light compare? Give five examples where you notice this.
31) A crash of thunder is heard 6 seconds after the flash of lightning. How far away was the flash of lightning? (The speed of sound in air is 330 m/s.)
32) If the sea bed is 600m down, how long will it take to receive a sonar echo from it? (The speed of sound in water is 1400 m/s.)
33) A bat sends out a squeak and receives the echo 0.45s later. How far away is the moth?
34) What aspect of EM waves determines their differing properties?
35) Sketch the EM spectrum with all its details. What happens when EM waves are absorbed?
36) Give full details of the uses of radio waves. How do the three different types get "around".
37) Give full details of the two main uses of microwaves, and the three main uses of infrared.
38) Give a sensible example of the use of visible light. What is its main use?
39) Detail two uses of UV light, one use of X-rays and three uses of gamma rays.
40) What harm will UV, X-rays and gamma rays do in _high_ doses? What about in _low_ doses?

The Solar System

You need to learn the _order_ of the planets, which is made easier by using the little jollyism below:

Mercury,	Venus,	Earth,	Mars,	(Asteroids),	Jupiter,	Saturn,	Uranus,	Neptune,	Pluto
(My	Very	Energetic	Maiden	Aunt	Just	Swam	Under	North	Pier)

The Asteroids are a belt of rocks orbiting between Mars and Jupiter.

MERCURY, _VENUS_, _EARTH_ and _MARS_ are known as the _INNER PLANETS_.
JUPITER, _SATURN_, _URANUS_, _NEPTUNE_ and _PLUTO_ are much further away and are the _OUTER PLANETS_.

The Planets Don't Give Out Light, They just Reflect The Sun's

1) You can _see_ some of the nearer planets with the _naked eye_ at night, e.g. Mars and Venus.
2) They look _just like stars_, but they are of course _totally different_.
3) Stars are _huge_ and _very far away_ and _give out_ lots of light.
   The planets are _smaller and nearer_ and they just _reflect the sunlight_ falling on them.
4) Planets always _orbit around stars_. In our Solar System the planets orbit the _Sun_ of course.
5) These orbits are all _slightly elliptical_ (elongated circles).
5) All the planets in our Solar System orbit in the _same plane_ except Pluto (as shown).
7) The _further_ the planet is from the Sun, the _longer_ its orbit takes (see next page).

The Sun is a Star, Giving Out All Types of EM Radiation

Sun

1) The Sun is at the _centre_ of the Solar System.
2) The Sun produces _massive amounts of heat and light_, created by _nuclear reactions_ deep inside it. It's _very hot_.
3) It gives out the _full spectrum_ of _electromagnetic radiation_.
4) This diagram shows how _huge_ the Sun is compared to the planets:

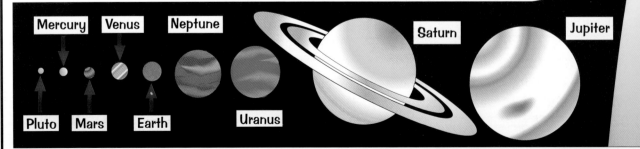

Mercury Venus Neptune Saturn Jupiter
Pluto Mars Earth Uranus

Learn The Planets — they can be quite illuminating...

Isn't the Solar System great! All those pretty coloured planets and all that big black empty space. You can look forward to one or two easy questions on the planets — or you might get two real horrors instead. Be ready, _learn_ all the _nitty gritty details_ till you know it all real good.

The Planets

Some Data on Planets which you Need to Kind of Know About

That doesn't mean you should learn every number, but you should definitely have a pretty good idea which planets are biggest, or furthest out etc. This table is a summary of the most important data on planets:

	PLANET	DIAMETER (km)	MASS	MEAN DIST. FROM SUN	ORBIT TIME
INNER PLANETS	MERCURY	4 800	0.05	58	88d
	VENUS	12 100	0.8 (Earth	108 (millions	225d d=Earth days
	EARTH	12 800	1.0 masses)	150 of km)	365d
	MARS	6 800	0.1	228	687d
OUTER PLANETS	JUPITER	143 000	318.0	778	12y
	SATURN	120 000	95.0	1430	29y y=Earth years
	URANUS	51 000	15.0	2870	84y
	NEPTUNE	49 000	17.0	4500	165y
	PLUTO	2 400	0.003	5900	248y

Gravity Is the Force which Keeps Everything in Orbit

1) _Gravity_ is a _force of attraction_ which acts between _all masses_.
2) With _very large masses_ like _stars_ and _planets_, the force is _very big_ and acts _a long way out_.
3) The _closer_ you get to a planet, the _stronger_ the _force of attraction_.
4) To _counteract_ this stronger gravity, the planet must move _faster_ and cover its orbit _quicker_.
5) _Comets_ are also held in _orbit_ by gravity, as are _moons_ and _satellites_ and _space stations_.

Comet

Comets Orbit the Sun, but have very Elongated Orbits

Comets only appear _every few years_ because their _orbits_ take them _very far from the Sun_ and then _back in close_, which is when _we_ see them. The Sun is _not at the centre_ of the orbit but _near to one end_ as shown.

Planets in the Night Sky Seem to Move across the Constellations

1) The stars in the sky form _fixed patterns_ called _constellations_.
2) These all stay _fixed_ in _relation to each other_ and simply "_rotate_" as the Earth spins.
3) The _planets_ look _just like stars_ except that they _wander_ across the constellations over periods of _days or weeks_, often going in the _opposite direction_.
4) Their position and movement depends on where they are _in their orbit_, compared to us.
5) This _peculiar movement of the planets_ made the _early astronomers_ realise that the Earth _wasn't the centre of the Universe_ after all, but was in fact just _the third rock from the Sun_. It's _very strong evidence_ for the _Sun-centred_ model of the Solar System.
6) Alas, the boys at _The Spanish Inquisition_ were less than keen on such heresy, and poor old _Copernicus_ had a pretty hard time of it for a while. In the end though, "_the truth will out_".

Learn This Page — but keep shtum to the boys in the Red Robes...

Planets are ace aren't they. There's all that exciting data to sort of be vaguely familiar with for a start. Then there's the fact that you can see one or two of them in the night sky, just by lifting your eyes to the heavens. _Learn_ all the other details on this page too, then _cover and scribble_.

The Cause of Day and Night

The Rotation of The Earth Causes Day and Night

1) The Earth is _constantly rotating_ in space. As the diagram shows, as the Earth _slowly rotates_, a point on the Earth's surface will slowly move from the _bright side_ in the _sunlight_ round into the _dark side_ out of the sun and then, as the Earth continues turning, eventually back into the sunshine again on the other side. This sequence describes _day-dusk-night-dawn_.
The "dusk" side of the Earth is hidden round the other side on this diagram:

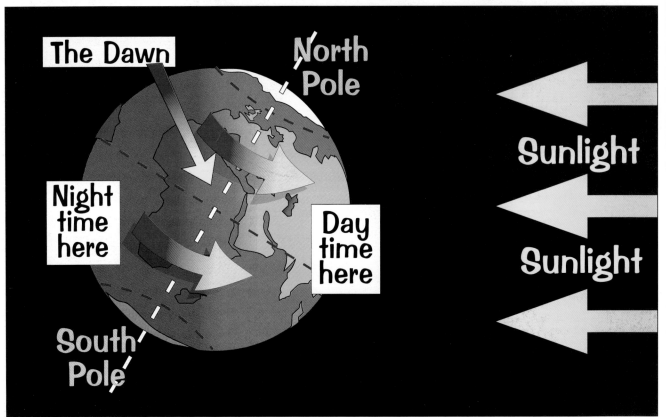

2) A _full rotation_ takes _24 hours_ of course — a full day. Next time you watch the _Sun set_, try to _imagine yourself_ helpless on that _big rotating ball_ as you move silently across the _twilight zone_ and into the _shadows_.
Note that there's _always somewhere_ on the Earth where it's _daytime_ and always somewhere where the _dawn is just breaking_, and always somewhere where the Sun is _just setting_ etc.

3) Also notice that because of the _tilt of the axis_, places in the _Northern Hemisphere_ are spending _much longer_ in the _sunshine_ than in the _shade_ (night time), whereas places in the _Southern Hemisphere_ are spending more time in the _dark_. This is only because of the _time of year_. The next page shows how the tilt affects us at _different times of the year_.

4) Also notice that the further towards the _Poles_ you get, the _longer_ the days are in _summer_ and the longer the _nights_ are in _winter_. Places _inside the arctic circle_ have _24 hours a day_ of sunlight for a few days in _mid summer_, whilst in _mid winter_ the Sun _never rises at all_.

5) At the _Equator_ by contrast, the length of day _never varies_ from one season to the next. It's always _12 hours of day_ and _12 hours of night_. The position of the _shadows_ shows all this.

Phew — to think we're all just helpless on a big rotating ball...

This is pretty interesting stuff really, but you've got to make sure you _really know it_ well enough to answer an Exam question on it. Practise by _sketching out the above diagram_ entirely from _memory_ and then _scribbling out the details_ to explain why the Sun seems to rise and set, etc.

The Cause of Years and Seasons

A Year is One Full Orbit of The Earth Around The Sun

1) The Earth _rotates on its own axis_ once every _24 hours_. That causes _day and night_ as the different sides turn to _face the Sun_.

2) At the same time though, the Earth is also _travelling very fast through space_ (at about 100,000 km/h in fact) racing around its _orbit of the Sun_. This is a _very long way_ and even at that speed it still takes it _365 days_ to get all the way round. That's _one full year_ of course.

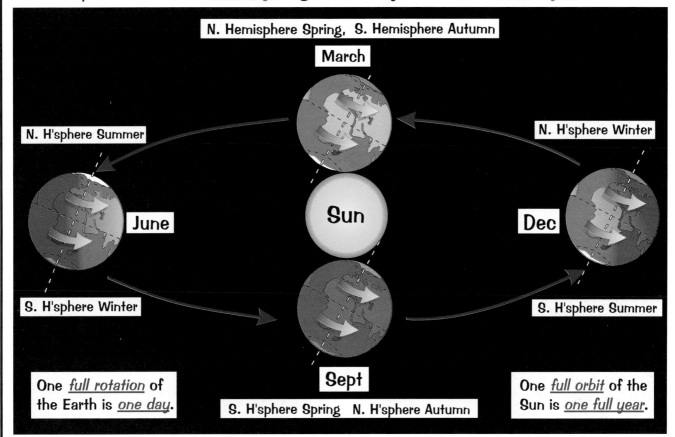

N. Hemisphere Spring, S. Hemisphere Autumn
March

N. H'sphere Summer

N. H'sphere Winter

June

Sun

Dec

S. H'sphere Winter

S. H'sphere Summer

One _full rotation_ of the Earth is _one day_.

Sept

S. H'sphere Spring   N. H'sphere Autumn

One _full orbit_ of the Sun is _one full year_.

The Seasons are Caused By The Tilt of the Earth's Axis

1) As the Earth _moves in its orbit_ around the Sun _the tilt of its axis_ causes the Northern and Southern Hemispheres to _alternate_ between having _long hours of daylight_ and _shorter days_.

2) The diagram _on the previous page_ shows the _Northern Hemisphere_ enjoying long days with long periods of time in the sunshine — i.e. _summer_.

3) The diagram _above_ shows _four different positions_ in the year with the North and South having _opposite seasons_ at all times.

4) When either hemisphere has _long days in the sun_ the _temperature rises_ and they have _summer_.

5) In the _winter_ it gets cold because they spend so much time _out of the sun_ exposed to the _cold dark blackness_ of space.

6) In _March_ and _September_, the axis is tilted _broadside_ to the Sun so _everywhere_, North and South, gets _12 hours of sunlight_ — except for Britain of course, where it will still be raining.

See Norway at Christmas — take a good torch...

This stuff about what causes the Sun to seem to "rise" and "set" and how the seasons are caused is surely irresistible-just-gotta-know-all-about-it kind of information, isn't it? Surely you must be filled with burning curiosity about it every time the dawn breaks — aren't you?

Moons and Satellites

Moons are Heavenly Bodies Which Orbit Planets

1) The Earth only has _one Moon_ of course, but some of the _other planets_ have _quite a few_.
2) We can only _see_ the Moon because it _reflects sunlight_.
3) The _phases of the Moon_ happen depending on _how much_ of the _illuminated side_ of the Moon we can _see_, as shown:

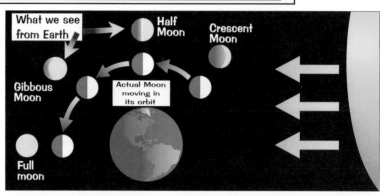

What we see from Earth — Half Moon — Crescent Moon — Gibbous Moon — Actual Moon moving in its orbit — Full moon

The Moon is Quite Near, The Sun is Big and Far Far Away

The Moon is pretty small but it's only about ½ million km away.

The Sun is huge but it's about 150 million km away.

Satellites Have Different Orbits for Different Jobs

Artificial satellites are put into fixed orbits around the Earth for _FOUR MAIN PURPOSES_:

1) Monitoring _Weather_
2) _Communications_, e.g. phone and TV.
3) _Space research_ e.g. the Hubble Telescope.
4) _Spying_ on baddies.

1) _High orbits_ are used for _communications_ to give _direct line of sight_ for the signal over _a large area_ of the Earth's surface.
2) _Low orbits_ are much better for _weather photos_ and _spying photos_, because the satellite needs to be _near enough_ to see what's going on.

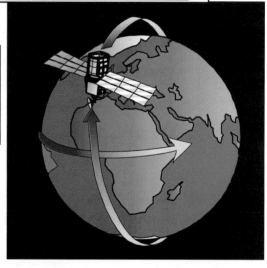

The Hubble Telescope has no Atmosphere in the way

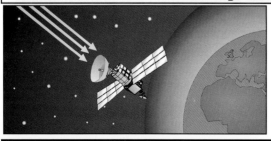

1) The _big advantage_ of having telescopes on _satellites_ is that they can look out into space _without_ the _distortion_ and _blurring_ caused by the Earth's _atmosphere_.
2) This allows _much greater detail_ to be seen of _distant stars_ and also the _planets_ in the Solar System.

Learn about Satellites — and look down on your friends...

You can actually see spy satellites on a nice dark clear night. They look like stars except they move quite fast in a dead straight line across the sky. _Learn all these details_ about the Moon and about satellites, ready for seizing juicy marks. Then _cover the page_ and _scribble it all down_.

The Universe

Stars and Solar Systems form from Clouds of Dust

1) _Stars form_ from _clouds of dust_ which _spiral in together_ due to _gravitational attraction_.
2) The gravity _compresses_ the matter so much that _intense heat_ develops and sets off _nuclear fusion reactions_ and the star then begins _emitting light_ and _other radiation_.
3) At the _same time_ that the star is forming, _other lumps_ may develop in the _spiralling dust clouds_ and these eventually gather together and form _planets_ which orbit _around the star_.

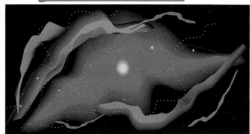

Our Sun is in The Milky Way Galaxy

1) The _Sun_ is one of _many millions_ of _stars_ which form the _Milky Way Galaxy_.
2) The _distance_ between neighbouring stars is usually _millions of times greater_ than the distance between _planets_ in our Solar System.
The Milky Way is _100,000 light years_ across.
3) _Gravity_ is of course the _force_ which keeps the stars _together_ in a _galaxy_ and, like most things in the Universe, the _galaxies all rotate_, kinda like a catherine wheel only _much slower_.
4) Our Sun is out towards the _end_ of one of the _spiral arms_ of the Milky Way galaxy.

The Whole Universe has More Than A Billion Galaxies

1) _Galaxies_ themselves are often _millions of times further apart_ than the _stars are_ within a galaxy.
2) So even the slowest amongst you will soon begin to realise that the Universe is _mostly empty space_ and is _really really big_. Ever been inside the NEC? Yeah? Well, it's even bigger than that.

A "Light-year" is NOT a Period of Time — it's a Distance

Try and remember this will you. A _light-year_ is just a very _big distance_ through space:

> **A LIGHT-YEAR is the DISTANCE that light travels IN ONE YEAR**

The _nearest star_ to us (apart from the Sun of course) is _4.2 light years_ away.
That means that the _light_ it gives off takes _4.2 years_ to _reach us_ here on Earth.
When you _look_ at that star in the sky, you're actually seeing what it was like _more than 4 years ago_. And considering light goes at _300,000,000 m/s_ (i.e. right round the Earth seven times in less than a second) you'll realise how _very very very far away_ those stars really are. Phew.

Galaxies, The Milky Way — it's just like a big chocolate factory...

More gripping facts about the Universe. It's just so big — look at those numbers: 1 light year is _9½ million million km_, one galaxy is _100,000_ of those across, and the Universe contains _billions_ of galaxies, all _millions_ of times further apart than 100,000 light years is. Man, _that's real big_.

Revision Summary for Section Four

The Universe is completely mindblowing in its own right. But surely the most mindblowing thing of all is the very fact that we are actually here, sitting and contemplating the truly outrageous improbability of our own existence. If your mind isn't blowing, then it hasn't sunk in yet. Think about it. 15 billion years ago there was a huge explosion, but there was no need for the whole chain of events to happen which allowed (or caused?) intelligent life to evolve and develop to the point where it became conscious of its own existence, not to mention the very disturbing unlikelihood of it all. But we have. We're here. Maaaan — is that freaky or what? The Universe could so easily have existed without conscious life ever evolving. Or come to that, the Universe needn't exist at all. Just black nothingness. So why does it exist? And why are we here? And why do we have to do so much revision? Who knows — but stop dreaming and get on with it.

1) What is the Solar System? What's right in the middle of the Solar System?
2) List the names of the nine planets in the right order, from the centre outwards.
3) What do planets look like in the night sky?
4) Which planets can be seen with the naked eye?
5) What's the big difference between planets and stars?
6) How does the Sun produce all its heat? What does the Sun give out?
7) Which is the biggest planet? Which is the smallest? Sketch the relative sizes of all of them.
8) What is it that keeps the planets in their orbits?
9) What other things are held in orbits apart from planets?
10) Sketch a diagram of a comet orbit.
11) What are constellations?
12) What do planets do in the constellations? Explain why they do this.
13) Who had trouble with the boys in the red robes? Why did he have such trouble?
14) Sketch a diagram to explain how day and night come about.
15) Explain exactly what is actually happening when you sit and watch the sun "set".
16) Which parts of the world have the longest days and which parts have the shortest days?
17) Which part of the Earth has similar lengths of day all year round?
18) Sketch a diagram to show how the seasons come about.
19) How long does one full rotation of the Earth take?
20) How long does it take for the Earth to complete one full orbit of the Sun?
21) When it's summer in Britain, what season are they having in Australia?
22) When it's spring in Australia, what season is it in Britain?
23) Sketch a diagram to explain the phases of the Moon.
24) How far away from the Earth is the Moon?
25) How far away from Earth is the Sun?
26) Explain why the Sun and Moon look to be about the same size in the sky.
27) What are natural satellites and artificial satellites?
28) What four things do we use artificial satellites for?
29) What kind of orbits are needed for communication satellites? Why?
30) What kind of orbits are needed for spy satellites? Why?
31) What is the Hubble telescope and where is it? What's the big idea there then?
32) What do stars and solar systems form from? What force causes it all to happen?
33) What is the Milky Way? Sketch it and show our Sun in relation to it.
34) What is the Universe made up of? How big is it?
35) What is a light year? How many km there are in one light year?
36) How long would it take to get to the nearest star (4.2 light years away) at 20,000 km/h?
37) How strange is the Universe? What's the most mindblowing thing ever?

The Ten Types of Energy

You should know all of these _well enough_ to list them _from memory_, including the examples:

1) Electrical Energy

— you get it whenever a _current_ flows.

2) Light Energy

— from the _Sun_, _light bulbs_, etc.

3) Sound Energy

— from _loudspeakers_ or anything _noisy_.

4) Kinetic Energy

— anything that's _moving_ has it.

Remember, the _kinetic energy_ of something depends both on **MASS** and **SPEED**.

The _more it weighs_ and the _faster it's going_, the _bigger_ its kinetic energy will be.

small mass, not fast low kinetic energy

big fast lorries Ltd

big mass, real fast high kinetic energy

5) Nuclear Energy

— released only from _nuclear reactions_.

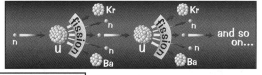

Kr · n · Ba · fission · U · Kr · n · Ba · fission · U · and so on...

6) Thermal Energy or Heat Energy

— _flows_ from _hot objects_ to colder ones.

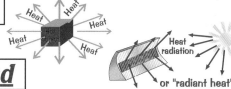

Heat

7) Radiant Heat Energy or Infra-Red

— given out as _EM radiation_ by _hot objects_.

Heat radiation or "radiant heat"

8) Gravitational Potential Energy

— possessed by anything which can _fall_.

What do you call a sheep with no eyes and no legs? · A cloud? · !

9) Elastic Potential Energy

— stretched _springs_, _elastic_, _rubber bands_, etc.

10) Chemical Energy

— possessed by _foods_, _fuels_ and _batteries_.

SUPREME

Potential- and Chemical- are forms of Stored Energy

The _last three_ above are forms of _stored energy_ because the energy is not obviously _doing_ anything, it's kind of _waiting to happen_, i.e. waiting to be turned into one of the _other_ forms.

Learn about Energy — and just keep working at it...

They're pretty keen on the different types of energy. You'll definitely get an Exam question on it, and if you learn all the stuff on this page and the next one, you should have it pretty well covered I'd think. _Learn, cover, scribble, check, learn, cover, scribble_, etc. etc. Enjoy.

Examples of Energy Transfer

They Like Giving Exam Questions on Energy Transfers

These are *very important examples*. You must *learn them* till you can repeat them all *easily*.

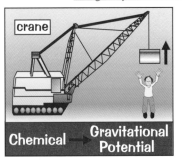

crane

Chemical → Gravitational Potential

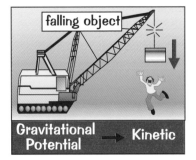

falling object

Gravitational Potential → Kinetic

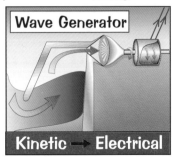

Wave Generator

Kinetic → Electrical

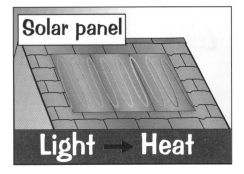

Solar panel

Light → Heat

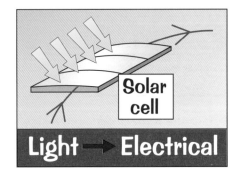

Solar cell

Light → Electrical

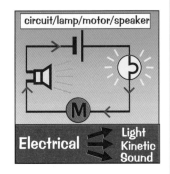

circuit/lamp/motor/speaker

Electrical → Light Kinetic Sound

Eating food / respiration

Chemical → Heat kinetic chemical

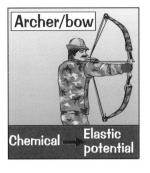

Archer/bow

Chemical → Elastic potential

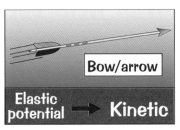

Bow/arrow

Elastic potential → Kinetic

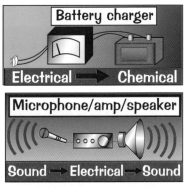

Battery charger

Electrical → Chemical

Microphone/amp/speaker

Sound → Electrical → Sound

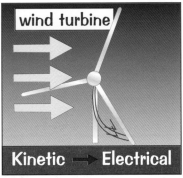

wind turbine

Kinetic → Electrical

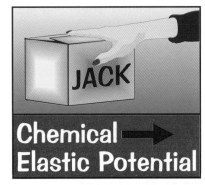

JACK

Chemical → Elastic Potential

JACK

Elastic Potential → Kinetic

And *DON'T FORGET* — *ALL types of ENERGY* are measured in *JOULES*

Transfer of Energy — it sure makes the world go round...

There are fourteen different examples on this page. They cover pretty well every type of energy transfer that you're likely to get. *Practise them* by looking at each picture whilst *keeping the red box covered*, and saying what kind of energy is changing into what other kind. That's pretty easy revision isn't it. It won't take long until you can do them all easily. *Enjoy*.

Work Done, Energy and Power

When a _force_ moves an _object_, _ENERGY IS TRANSFERRED_ and _WORK IS DONE_

That statement sounds far more complicated than it needs to. Try this:

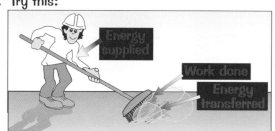

1) Whenever something _moves_, something else is providing some sort of _"effort"_ to move it.
2) The thing putting the _effort_ in needs a _supply of energy_ (like _fuel_ or _food_ or _electricity_ etc.).
3) It then does _"work"_ by _moving_ the object — and one way or another it _transfers the energy_ it receives (as fuel) into _other forms_.
4) Whether this energy is transferred "_usefully_" (e.g. by _lifting a load_) or is "_wasted_" (e.g. lost as _friction_), you can still say that "_work is done_". Just like Batman and Bruce Wayne, "_work done_" and "_energy transferred_" are indeed "_one and the same_".   (And they're both in _Joules_.)

It's Just _Another Trivial Formula:_

Work Done = Force × Distance

Whether the force is _friction_ or _weight_ or _tension in a rope_, it's always the same. To find how much _energy_ has been _transferred_ (in Joules), you just multiply the _force in N_ by the _distance moved in m_. Easy as that. I'll show you...

EXAMPLE: Some hooligan kids drag an old tractor tyre 5m over rough ground. They pull with a total force of 340N. Find the energy transferred.
ANSWER: Wd = F×d = 340 × 5 = _1700J_.   Phew — easy peasy isn't it?

Power is the "Rate of Doing Work" — i.e. how much per second

POWER is _not_ the same thing as _force_, nor _energy_. A _powerful_ machine is not necessarily one which can exert a strong _force_ (though it usually ends up that way).
A _POWERFUL_ machine is one which transfers _A LOT OF ENERGY IN A SHORT SPACE OF TIME_. This is the _very easy formula_ for power:

$$\text{Power} = \frac{\text{Work done}}{\text{Time taken}}$$

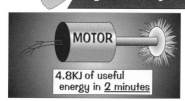

EXAMPLE: A motor transfers 4.8kJ of useful energy in 2 minutes. Find its power output.
ANSWER: P = Wd / t = 4,800/120 = 40W (or 40 J/s)
 (Note that the kJ had to be turned into J, and the minutes into seconds.)

Power is Measured in Watts (or J/s)

The proper unit of power is the _Watt_.   _One Watt = 1 Joule of energy transferred per second_.
Power means 'how much energy _per second_", so _Watts_ are the same as "_Joules per second_" (J/s).
Don't ever say "watts per second" — it's _nonsense_.

Revise work done — what else...

"_Energy transferred_" and "_work done_" are the same thing. I wonder how many times I need to say that before you'll remember.   Power is "_work done divided by time taken_". I wonder how many times you've got to see that before you realise you're supposed to _learn it_ as well...

Conservation of Energy

There are Two Types of "Energy Conservation"

Try and get your head round the difference between these two will you.

1) "_ENERGY CONSERVATION_" is all about _using less fossil fuels_ because of the damage it does and because they might _run out_. That's all _environmental stuff_, and it's fairly trivial, on a _cosmic scale_.

2) The "_PRINCIPLE OF THE CONSERVATION OF ENERGY_" on the other hand is one of the _major cornerstones_ of modern Physics. It's an _all-pervading principle_ which governs the workings of the _entire Physical Universe_. If this principle were not so, then life as we know it would simply cease to be.

3) Got it now? Good. _Well don't forget_.

The Principle of the Conservation of Energy _can be stated thus:_

> ### ENERGY can never be _CREATED_ nor _DESTROYED_
> ### — it's only ever _CONVERTED_ from one form to another.

Another _important principle_ which you need to _learn_ is this one:

> ### Energy is _ONLY USEFUL_ when it's _CONVERTED_ from one form to another.

Most Energy Transfers Involve Some Losses, as Heat

1) _Useful devices_ are only _useful_ because they _convert energy_ from _one form_ to _another_.

2) In doing so, some of the useful _input energy_ is always _lost or wasted_ as _heat_.

3) The _less energy_ that is _wasted_, the _more efficient_ the device is said to be.

4) The _energy flow diagram_ is pretty much the same for _all devices_. You _MUST_ learn this _BASIC ENERGY FLOW DIAGRAM_:

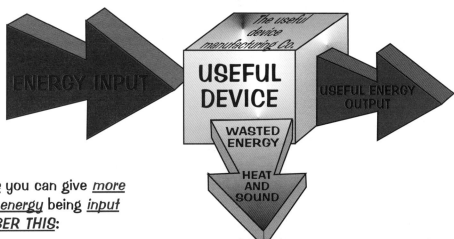

ENERGY INPUT → The useful device manufacturing Co. USEFUL DEVICE → USEFUL ENERGY OUTPUT / WASTED ENERGY HEAT AND SOUND

For any _specific example_ you can give _more detail_ about the _types of energy_ being _input_ and _output_, but _REMEMBER THIS_:

> ### _NO_ device is 100% efficient
> ### and the _WASTED ENERGY_ is always _dissipated_ as _HEAT_ and _SOUND_.

Electric heaters are the _exception_ to this. They're _100% efficient_ because _all_ the electricity is converted to "_useful_" heat. _What else could it become?_ Ultimately, _all_ energy _ends up as heat energy_. If you use an electric drill, it gives out _various types_ of energy but they all quickly end up as _heat_. That's an important thing to realise. So realise it — and _never forget it_.

Learn about energy dissipation — but keep your cool...

The thing about loss of energy is it's always the same — it always disappears as heat and sound, and even the sound ends up as heat pretty quickly. So when they ask "Why is the input energy more than the output energy?", the answer is always the same... _Learn and enjoy_.

Efficiency of Machines

A _machine_ is a device which turns _one type of energy_ into _another_.
The _efficiency_ of any device is defined as:

$$\text{Efficiency} = \frac{\text{USEFUL Energy OUTPUT}}{\text{TOTAL Energy INPUT}}$$

$$\frac{\text{Energy out}}{\text{Efficiency} \times \text{Energy in}}$$

You can give efficiency as a _fraction_, _decimal_ or _percentage_, i.e. ¾ or 0.75 or 75%.

Come on! — Efficiency is Really Simple...

1) You find how much energy is _supplied_ to a machine. (The Total Energy _INPUT_)
2) You find how much _useful energy_ the machine _delivers_. (The Useful Energy _OUTPUT_)
   They either tell you this directly or they tell you how much it _wastes_ as heat/sound.
3) Either way, you get those _two important numbers_ and then just _divide_ the _smaller one_ by the _bigger one_ to get a value for _efficiency_ somewhere between _0 and 1_ (or _0 and 100%_). Easy.
4) The other way they might ask it is to tell you the _efficiency and the input energy_ and ask for the _energy output_. The best way to tackle that is to _learn_ this _other version_ of the formula:

USEFUL ENERGY OUTPUT = _Efficiency_ × **TOTAL Energy INPUT**

Five Important Examples on Efficiency for you to Learn

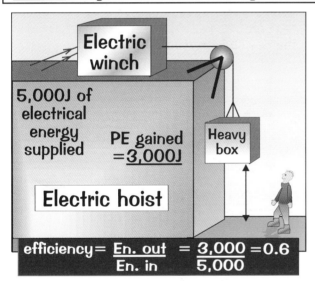

Electric winch

5,000J of electrical energy supplied

PE gained = **3,000J**

Heavy box

Electric hoist

$$\text{efficiency} = \frac{\text{En. out}}{\text{En. in}} = \frac{3,000}{5,000} = 0.6$$

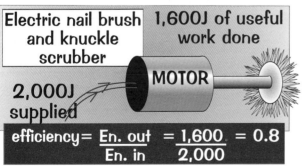

Electric nail brush and knuckle scrubber

1,600J of useful work done

MOTOR

2,000J supplied

$$\text{efficiency} = \frac{\text{En. out}}{\text{En. in}} = \frac{1,600}{2,000} = 0.8$$

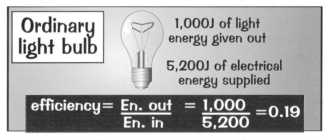

Ordinary light bulb

1,000J of light energy given out

5,200J of electrical energy supplied

$$\text{efficiency} = \frac{\text{En. out}}{\text{En. in}} = \frac{1,000}{5,200} = 0.19$$

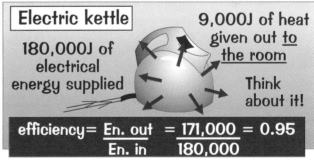

Electric kettle

180,000J of electrical energy supplied

9,000J of heat given out _to the room_

Think about it!

$$\text{efficiency} = \frac{\text{En. out}}{\text{En. in}} = \frac{171,000}{180,000} = 0.95$$

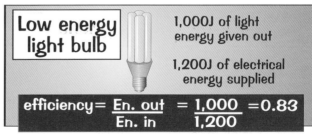

Low energy light bulb

1,000J of light energy given out

1,200J of electrical energy supplied

$$\text{efficiency} = \frac{\text{En. out}}{\text{En. in}} = \frac{1,000}{1,200} = 0.83$$

Learn about energy transfer — but do it efficiently...

Efficiency is another hideously simple concept. It's a big funny-looking word I grant you, but that doesn't mean it's tricky. Let's face it, efficiency's a blummin' doddle — divide E_{out} by E_{in} and there it is, done. Geesh. _Learn the page_, then _cover it up_ and _scribble down_ what you know.

Heat Transfer

It's *funny old stuff* really, heat is.

Heat Energy Causes Molecules to Move Faster

1) *Heat energy* causes *gas and liquid* molecules to move around *faster*, and causes particles in solids to *vibrate more rapidly*.
2) When particles move *faster* it shows up as a *rise in temperature*.
3) This extra *kinetic energy* in the particles tends to get *dissipated* to the *surroundings*.
4) In other words the *heat energy* tends to *flow away* from a hotter object to its *cooler surroundings*.
But then you *knew that already*, I would hope.

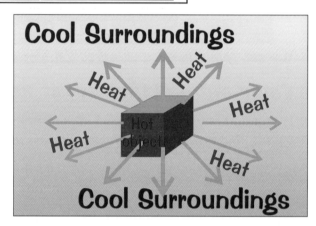

If there's a *DIFFERENCE IN TEMPERATURE* between two places then *HEAT WILL FLOW* between them.

There are Four Ways That Heat Can Be Transferred

1) It's one thing to realise that a *difference in temperature* means *heat will flow*.
2) It's quite another to remember that there are *four completely different* ways that the *heat can flow*.
3) But you do need to *know them*. Real good in fact.
The next few pages tell you *all about them*, but make sure you *learn their names* first:

**1) Conduction
2) Convection
3) Radiation
4) Evaporation**

You normally only consider the *first three* of these. Evaporation isn't as common as the others so you usually *ignore it*.

Evaporation is One Way That Heat Can be Lost

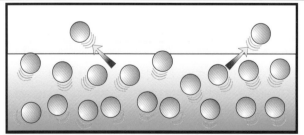

1) In a *liquid* the *hottest* particles are moving the *fastest*.
2) *Fast moving* particles near the liquid *surface* are likely to *break free* of the liquid and *evaporate*.
3) Only the *fastest* particles will achieve this, leaving the *slower* "*cooler*" particles *behind*.
4) This *lowers the average energy* of the particles left in the liquid and so *the liquid as a whole* becomes *cooler*.
5) It then *takes in heat* from its surroundings and thereby *cools* whatever it's in *contact* with. This is how *sweating* works.
6) *Evaporation* will *only happen* if there's an *exposed liquid surface* for the "hot" molecules to escape from. A sealed bottle of water will *not* lose any heat by *evaporation*.

Heat Transfer

There are _three distinct methods_ of heat transfer: _CONDUCTION_, _CONVECTION_ and _RADIATION_.
To answer Exam questions you _must_ use those _three key words_ in just the _right places_,
And that means you need to know _exactly what they are_, and all the _differences_ between them.

Conduction, Convection _and Radiation Compared_

These differences are _really important_ —
make sure you _LEARN them_:

1) _Conduction_ occurs mainly in _solids_.
2) _Convection_ occurs mainly in _gases and liquids_.
3) Gases and liquids are _very poor conductors_ — convection is usually the _dominant process_. Where convection _can't_ occur, the heat transfer by _conduction_ is _very slow indeed_, as the diagram of the immersion heater shows. This is a _classic example_, so it's a pretty good plan to _learn it_.

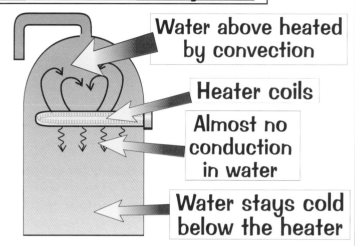

Water above heated by convection

Heater coils

Almost no conduction in water

Water stays cold below the heater

4) _Radiation_ travels through anything _see-through_ including a _vacuum_.
5) _Heat Radiation_ is given out by _anything_ which is _warm or hot_.

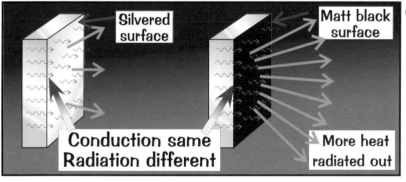

Silvered surface

Matt black surface

Conduction same Radiation different

More heat radiated out

6) The _amount_ of heat radiation which is _absorbed or emitted_ depends on the _colour_ and _texture_ of the _surface_.
But don't forget, _convection and conduction_ are _totally unaffected_ by surface colour or texture. A _shiny white_ surface _conducts_ just as well as a _matt black_ one.

Convection Heaters _and "Radiators" — Watch out!_

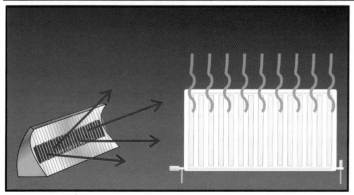

1) A "_radiator_" strictly should be something that _glows red_ and gives most heat out as _radiation_, like a _coal fire_ or an _electric bar radiator_.
2) Central heating "_radiators_" have the _wrong name_ really, because they're not like that at all. They give _most_ heat out as _convection currents_ of warm rising air. This is what a "_convector heater_" does.

Learn the facts on heat transfer — but don't get a sweat on...

Phew, no more numbers and formulae, now we're back to good old straightforward factual learning again. Much less confusing — but no less of a challenge, it has to be said. You've really got to make a fair old effort to get the three key processes of heat transfer all sorted out in your head so that you know exactly what they are and when they occur. _Learn and grin_.

Conduction of Heat

Conduction of Heat — Occurs Mainly in Solids

Conduction of heat happens because the *"hot"* *vibrating particles* pass on their *extra vibrational energy* to the "cooler" atoms next to them, which aren't vibrating as much.

1) *Conduction* is the simplest form of *heat transfer* — it's certainly the easiest to understand.
2) The *big mistake* people make though, is to think that "*flow of heat*" just means conduction.
3) You've got to learn that "*flow of heat*" also takes two other forms: *convection* and *radiation*.
4) Conduction is the *usual way* that heat travels through *solids*.
5) It's *pretty quick in metals*. It's *pretty slow* in everything else.

CONDUCTION OF HEAT is the process where VIBRATING PARTICLES pass on their EXTRA VIBRATION ENERGY to NEIGHBOURING PARTICLES.

This process continues *throughout the solid* and gradually the *extra vibrational energy* (or *heat*) is passed all the way through the solid, causing a *rise in temperature* at the other side.

Metals are Good Conductors — Non-metals are Good Insulators

1) The *normal process of conduction* as shown above is always *very slow*.
2) But in most *non-metal solids* it's the *only* way that heat can pass through.
3) So *non-metals*, such as *plastic*, *wood*, *rubber* etc. are very good *insulators*.
4) Non-metal *gases and liquids* are even *worse conductors*, as you will slowly begin to realise if I say it often enough. *Metals*, on the other hand, are all *very good conductors*.

Metals always FEEL hotter or colder to the touch because they conduct the heat into or out of your hand very quickly

1) You'll notice if a *spade* is left out in the *sun* that the *metal part* will always *FEEL* much *hotter* than the *wooden handle*. *BUT IT ISN'T HOTTER* — it just *conducts* the heat *into your hand* much quicker than the wood, so your hand *heats up* much *quicker* when you touch it, and that *feels hotter*, of course.

Ooh! Ow! It's hot — or perhaps it's not.

2) In *cold weather* it's the opposite — the *metal bits* of a spade, or anything else, always *feel colder* because they *take the heat away* from your hand quicker. But they're *NOT COLDER*... try and remember that because they quite like to ask questions about it.

Good conductors are always metals? — what about Henry Wood...

Well sure, conduction is pretty easy, but that doesn't mean they can't ask some fairly tricky questions on it if they want to. What you need to do is make sure you've learnt all the little picky details on this page. When you think you have, *cover the page* and *see what you know*.

Convection of Heat

Gases and liquids are usually free to _slosh about_ — and that allows them to transfer heat by _convection_, which is a _much more effective process_ than conduction.

Convection of Heat — Liquids and Gases Only

Convection simply _can't happen in solids_ because the particles _can't move_.

> _CONVECTION_ occurs when the more energetic particles _MOVE_ from the _hotter region_ to the _cooler region_ — _AND TAKE THEIR HEAT ENERGY WITH THEM_

When the _more energetic_ (i.e. _hotter_) particles get somewhere _cooler_ they then _transfer their energy_ by the usual process of _collisions_ which warm up the surroundings.

Natural Convection Currents Are Caused By Changes in Density

The diagram shows a _typical convection current_. Make sure you _learn_ all the bits about _expansion_ and _density changes_ which _cause_ the convection current. It's all worth _juicy marks_ in the Exam.

2 The heated air expands and becomes less dense. It therefore rises.

4 As air cools, it contracts and becomes more dense and falls.

1 The land heats up quickly in the sun and heats the air above it.

3 Cool air rushes in to replace the rising warm air, creating an onshore sea breeze.

Natural Convection Produces Ocean Currents

1) The ocean _near the Equator_ is heated _most strongly_ by the Sun and the warmed water _expands slightly_, becomes _less dense_ and _rises_ to the surface. It then _pushes outwards_ to be replaced by more warmed water _pushing up_ from underneath. These _warm surface currents_ can travel for _hundreds of miles_.
2) The same thing happens in a beaker but on a smaller scale.

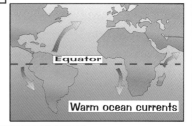

Equator

Warm ocean currents

Forced Convection is Used to Cool Machinery and Us

1) _Forced convection_ is simply where you have a _fan_ or _pump_ making the gas or liquid _move around much faster_.
2) In a _car engine_ the _water pump_ pushes the water around quickly to _transfer heat_ away from the _engine_ and get rid of it at the _radiator_. That's _forced convection_.

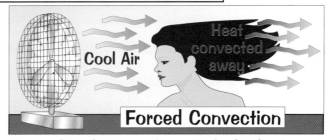

Cool Air

Heat convected away

Forced Convection

3) Inside, we use _cooling fans_ to blow air over us to _cool us down_, or alternatively _fan heaters_ blow warm air around the room _much quicker_ than the natural convection currents would.

Convection Currents — easy as a summer evening breeze...

Oi! Watch out! It's another pair of Physics words that look so much alike that half of you think they're the same word. Look: CONVECTION. See, it's different from CONDUCTION. Tricky that one isn't it. Just like reflection and refraction. Not just a different word though, convection is a _totally different process_ too. Make sure you learn exactly why it isn't like conduction.

Heat Radiation

Heat radiation can also be called _infra-red radiation_, and it consists purely of electromagnetic waves of a certain frequency. It's just below visible light in the _electromagnetic spectrum_.

Heat Radiation Can Travel Through Vacuum

Heat radiation is _different_ from the _other two methods_ of heat transfer in quite a few ways:
1) It travels in _straight lines_ at the _speed of light_.
2) It travels through _vacuum_. This is the _only way_ that heat can reach us _from the Sun_.
3) It can be very effectively _reflected away again_ by a _silver surface_.
4) It only travels through _transparent media_, like _air_, _glass_ and _water_.
5) Its behaviour is _strongly dependent_ on _surface colour and texture_. This _definitely isn't so_ for conduction and convection.
6) No _particles_ are involved. It's _transfer of heat energy_ purely by _waves_.

Emission and Absorption of Heat Radiation

1) _All objects_ are _continually_ emitting and absorbing _heat radiation_.
2) The _hotter_ they are the _more_ heat radiation they _emit_.
3) _Cooler ones_ around them will _absorb_ this heat radiation. You can _feel_ this _heat radiation_ if you stand near something _hot_ like a fire.

Just a smidge of heat radiation

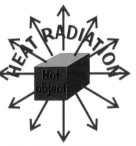

It Depends An Awful Lot on Surface Colour _and_ Texture

1) _Dark matt surfaces_ _ABSORB_ heat radiation falling on them _much more strongly_ than _bright glossy surfaces_, such as _gloss white_ or _silver_. They _also emit_ heat radiation _much more_ too.
2) _Silvered surfaces_ _REFLECT_ nearly all heat radiation falling on them.
3) In the lab there are several fairly dull experiments to _demonstrate the effects of surface_ on _emission and absorption of heat radiation_. Here are two of the most gripping:

Leslie's Cube
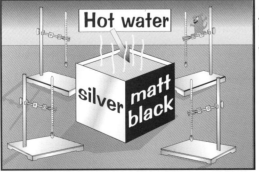

The _matt black_ side _EMITS_ most heat so it's that thermometer which gets _hottest_.

The _matt black_ surface _ABSORBS_ _most heat_ so its wax _melts_ first and the ball bearing _drops_.

The Melting Wax Trick
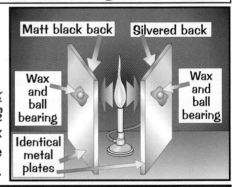

Revise Heat Radiation — absorb as much as you can, anyway...

The main thing to learn here is that heat radiation is strongly affected by the colour and texture of surfaces. Don't forget that the other two types of heat transfer, conduction and convection, are not affected by surface colour and texture _at all_. Heat radiation is totally different from conduction and convection. _Learn_ all the details on this page, then _cover it up_ and _scribble_.

Applications of Heat Transfer

Good Conductors and Good Insulators

1) _All metals_ are _good conductors_. e.g. iron, brass, aluminium, copper, gold, silver, etc.
2) All _non-metals_ are good _insulators_.
3) Gases and liquids are truly _abysmal conductors_ (but are great _convectors_ don't forget).
4) The _best insulators_ are ones which _trap pockets of air_. If the air _can't move_, it _can't_ transfer heat by _convection_ and so the heat has to _conduct_ very slowly through the _pockets of air_, as well as the material in between. This really slows it down _bigstyle_.
   This is how _clothes_ and _blankets_ and _loft insulation_ and _cavity wall insulation_ and _polystyrene cups_ and _pretty woollen mittens_ and _little furry animals_ and _fluffy yellow ducklings_ work.

Insulation should also take account of Heat Radiation

1) _Silvered finishes_ are highly effective _insulation_ against heat transfer by _radiation_.
2) This can work _both ways_, either keeping heat radiation _out_ or keeping heat _in_.

KEEPING HEAT RADIATION OUT:	KEEPING HEAT IN:
Spacesuits	Shiny metal kettles
Cooking foil on the turkey	Survival blankets
Thermos flasks	Thermos flasks (again)

3) _Matt black_ is rarely used for its thermal properties of _absorbing_ and _emitting_ heat radiation.
4) It's only _useful_ where you want to _get rid of heat_, e.g. the _cooling fins_ or _radiator_ on an engine.

The Thermos Flask — The Ultimate in Insulation

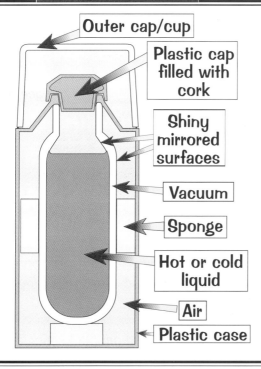

Outer cap/cup
Plastic cap filled with cork
Shiny mirrored surfaces
Vacuum
Sponge
Hot or cold liquid
Air
Plastic case

1) The glass bottle is _double-walled_ with a _thin vacuum_ between the two walls. This stops _all conduction and convection_ through the _sides_.
2) The walls either side of the vacuum are _silvered_ to keep heat loss by _radiation_ to a _minimum_.
3) The bottle is supported using _insulating foam_. This minimises heat _conduction_ to or from the _outer_ glass bottle.
4) The _stopper_ is made of _plastic_ and filled with _cork or foam_ to reduce any _heat conduction_ through it.
5) In _Exam questions_ you must _always_ say which form of heat transfer is involved at any point, either _conduction_, _convection_ or _radiation_. An answer such as: _"The vacuum stops heat getting out"_ will get you _no marks at all_.

Heat Transfer and Insulation — keep taking it all in..

There's a lot more to insulation that you first realise. That's because there are _three ways_ that heat can be transferred, and so effective heat insulation has to deal with _all three_, of course. The venerable Thermos Flask is the classic example of all-in-one-full-blown insulation. _Learn it_.

Keeping Buildings Warm

Loft Insulation
Initial Cost: £200
Annual Saving: £50
Payback time: _4 years_

Hot Water Tank Jacket
Initial Cost: £10
Annual Saving: £15
Payback time: _1 year_

Thermostatic Controls
Initial Cost: £100
Annual Saving: £20
Payback time: _5 years_

Double Glazing
Initial Cost: £3,000
Annual Saving: £60
Payback time: _50 years_

Cavity Wall Insulation
Initial Cost: £500
Annual Saving: £70
Payback time: _7 years_

Draught-proofing
Initial Cost: £50
Annual Saving: £50
Payback time: _1 year_

Effectiveness and Cost-effectiveness are not the same...

1) The figures above are all in the right "ball park", but of course it'll _vary_ from house to house.
2) The _cheaper_ methods of insulation tend to be a _lot_ more _cost-effective_ than the pricier ones.
3) The ones that save the _most money each year_ could be considered the most "_effective_", i.e. _cavity wall insulation_. How _cost-effective_ it is depends on what _time-scale_ you're looking at.
4) If you _subtract_ the _annual saving_ from the _initial cost_ repeatedly then _eventually_ the one with the _biggest annual saving_ must always come out as the winner, if you think about it.
5) But you might sell the house (or die) before that happens. If instead you look at it over say, a _five year period_ then the cheap and cheerful _draught-proofing_ wins. Who's to say?
6) But _double glazing_ is always _by far_ the _least cost-effective_, which is kinda comical, considering.

Know Which Types of Heat Transfer are Involved:

1) _CAVITY WALL INSULATION_ — foam squirted into the gap between the bricks reduces _convection_ and _radiation_ across the gap.
2) _LOFT INSULATION_ — a thick layer of fibre glass wool laid out across the whole loft floor reduces _conduction_ and _radiation_ into the roof space from the ceiling.
3) _DRAUGHT PROOFING_ — strips of foam and plastic around doors and windows stop draughts of cold air blowing in, i.e. they reduce heat loss due to _convection_.
4) _DOUBLE GLAZING_ — two layers of glass with an air gap reduce _conduction_ and _radiation_.
5) _THERMOSTATIC RADIATOR VALVES_ — these simply prevent the house being _over-warmed_.
6) _HOT WATER TANK JACKET_ — lagging such as fibre glass wool reduces _conduction_ and _radiation_ from the hot water tank.
7) _THICK CURTAINS_ — big bits of cloth you pull across the window to stop people looking in at you, but also to reduce heat loss by _conduction_ and _radiation_.

They don't seem to have these problems in Spain...

Remember, the most _effective_ insulation measure is the one which keeps the most heat in, (biggest annual saving). If your house had no roof, then a roof would be the most _effective_ measure, would it not! But _cost-effectiveness_ depends very much on the _time-scale_ involved.

Sources of Energy

The Sun Provides Most Of Our Energy

1) _The Sun_ is the _ultimate source_ for _nearly all_ of the energy available to us.
2) It generates its energy by _nuclear fusion reactions_ deep inside it.
3) This _energy_ is given off as _EM waves_ which reach us here on Earth as _light and heat radiation_.
4) On the next page are listed the _twelve_ main sources of _energy_. _Nine_ of those twelve _wouldn't be here at all_ if it wasn't for the Sun providing the _energy_ in the _first place_.
5) You need to know the five _energy transfer chains_ which _start_ from the _Sun_ and _end_ in those _nine types of energy source_. Here they are:

1) Sun's Energy ➡ Wood and Food

Sun ➡ _light energy_ ➡ _plants_ ➡ _photosynthesis_ ➡ BIOMASS (wood) or FOOD.

2) Sun's Energy ➡ Fossil Fuels

Sun ➡ _light energy_ ➡ _photosynthesis_ ➡ _dead plants/animals_ ➡ FOSSIL FUELS.

3) Sun's Energy ➡ Wind Power and Wave Power

Sun ➡ _heats atmosphere_ ➡ _creates WINDS_ ➡ _and therefore WAVES too._

4) Sun's Energy ➡ Hydro-electricity

Sun ➡ _heating sea water_ ➡ _clouds_ ➡ _rain_ ➡ HYDRO-ELECTRICITY.

5) Sun's Energy ➡ Solar Power

Sun ➡ _light energy_ ➡ SOLAR POWER.

Nuclear, Geothermal and Tidal Energy

These Energy Sources Do NOT Originate in the Sun

These are the _three sources of energy_ which are _not dependent_ on the _Sun_ being there.
1) _Nuclear power_ comes from the energy _locked up_ in the _nuclei of atoms_.
2) _Nuclear decay_ also creates some of the heat _inside the Earth_ for _geothermal energy_, though this happens _much slower_ than in a nuclear reactor. A lot of the _heat inside the Earth_ is actually _left over_ from when it first _formed_ about _five billion_ years ago! Phew.
3) _Tides_ are caused by the _gravitational attraction_ of the _Moon_ (and _Sun_) pulling the sea about.

Stop fuelling around and learn this stuff properly...

There's quite a few details here on sources of energy. In the Exam they could test you on any of them, so I guess _you just gotta learn 'em all_. This is the only page with those jazzy arrows actually in between words, which is quite a novelty. There you go then, _life isn't all bad_.

The Two Basic Types of Energy Resource

There are _twelve_ different types of _energy resource_.
They fit into _two broad types_: _RENEWABLE_ and _NON-RENEWABLE_. Learn all about them:

Comparison of Renewables and Non-Renewables

1) They're quite likely to give you an Exam question asking you to "_evaluate_" or "_discuss_" the _relative merits_ of generating power by _renewable_ and _non-renewable_ resources.
2) The way to _get the marks_ is to simply list the _pros and cons_ of each method.
3) Full details are given on the next few pages, but there are some _clear generalisations_ you should _definitely learn_.
4) Make sure you can _write down_ all of the _advantages and disadvantages_ of both types of resource as listed below — _all from memory_:

Renewable Resources

These Will Never Run Out
1) _WIND_
2) _WAVES_
3) _TIDES_
4) _HYDRO-ELECTRICITY_
5) _SOLAR_
6) _GEOTHERMAL_
7) _FOOD_
8) _BIOMASS (WOOD)_

Non-renewable Resources

These will All Run Out One Day
1) _COAL_
2) _OIL_
3) _NATURAL GAS_
4) _NUCLEAR FUELS_ (_uranium_ and _plutonium_)

   (i.e. the _three fossil fuels_ and _nuclear_)

Advantages

1) There is _no pollution_.
2) They will _never run out_.
3) They _do not damage the environment_ (except visually).
4) There are _no fuel costs_, although the initial costs can be high.

Disadvantages

1) They are all very _polluting_.
2) They are _running out_ quite quickly and will _run out_ completely one day.
3) They all do _damage to the environment_ — _mining or drilling_, _transportation_ of fuels, and _atmospheric pollution_. See opposite page.
4) Obtaining the _fuel_ is _expensive_.

Disadvantages

1) They usually require _large areas of land_ or water and often _spoil the landscape_.
2) They are basically _unreliable_ because most of them depend on the _weather_. They don't always deliver energy _when it's needed_.
3) They _don't provide much energy_.

Advantages

1) The _power stations_ don't take up much _land_ and _don't_ spoil too much _landscape_.
2) They give very _reliable_ output, entirely _independent of the weather_. They can always deliver energy _just when it's needed_.
3) They all provide very _high_ output, and they can provide _all our energy needs_ at present.

Learn about energy resources— it's all good clean fun...

Make sure you learn _all_ of this summary comparing renewables and non-renewables. You should notice that each advantage of one type is matched by a corresponding disadvantage of the other type. So if you _learn one side_, you should be able to _write down the other_. Enjoy.

Non-Renewable Energy Resources

1) _MOST_ of the electricity we use is _generated_ from the four _NON-RENEWABLE_ sources of energy (_coal_, _oil_, _gas_ and _nuclear_) in _big power stations_.
2) These power stations are all _pretty much the same_ apart from the _boiler_.
3) You should _LEARN_ the _basic features_ of the _typical power station_ shown here:

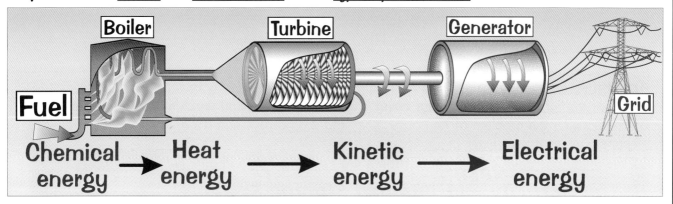

Boiler   Turbine   Generator

Fuel   Grid

Chemical energy → Heat energy → Kinetic energy → Electrical energy

Nuclear Reactors are Just Fancy Boilers

1) A _nuclear power station_ is mostly the same as the one shown above, where _heat is produced_ in a _boiler_ to make _steam_ to drive the _turbines_ etc.
2) The only difference is in the _boiler_, which is just a tadge more _complicated_.

Environmental Problems With The Use Of Non-Renewables

1) _All three fossil fuels_ (coal, oil and gas) release CO_2 which is causing _The Greenhouse Effect_.
2) Coal and oil also cause _acid rain_. This is now being reduced by _cleaning up the emissions_.
3) _Coal mining_ makes a _mess_ of the _landscape_, especially "_open-cast mining_".
4) _Oil spillages_ cause _serious environmental problems_. We try to avoid it, but it'll always happen.
5) _Nuclear power_ is clean but the _nuclear waste_ is very _dangerous_ and difficult to _dispose of_.
6) Nuclear _fuel_ (i.e. uranium) is _cheap_ but the _overall cost_ of nuclear power is _high_ due to the cost of the _power plant_ and final _de-commissioning_.
7) _Nuclear power_ always carries the risk of _major catastrophe_ like the _Chernobyl disaster_.

The Non-Renewables Need to be Conserved

1) When the _fossil fuels eventually RUN OUT_ we will _have_ to use _other forms_ of energy.
2) More importantly however, fossil fuels are also _a very useful source of chemicals_, (especially crude oil), which will be _hard to replace_ when they are all gone.
3) To stop the fossil fuels _running out so quickly_ there are _two things_ we can do:

1) Use Less Energy by Being More Efficient With it:

    (i) Better _insulation_ of buildings,
    (ii) Turning _lights and other things OFF_ when not needed,
    (iii) Making everyone drive _spiddly little cars_ with spacky little engines.

2) Use More Of The Renewable Sources Of Energy

as detailed on the following pages.

Learn about the non-renewables — before it's too late...

Make sure you realise that we generate most of our electricity from the four non-renewables, and that the power stations are all pretty much the same, as exemplified by the above diagram. Also make sure you know all the problems about them and why we should use less of them.

Wind Power and Hydroelectric Power

Wind Power — Lots of Little Wind Turbines

1) This involves putting _lots of windmills_ (wind turbines) up in _exposed places_ like on _moors_ or round _coasts_.
2) Each wind turbine has its own _generator_ inside it so the electricity is generated _directly_ from the _wind_ turning the _blades_, which _turn the generator_.
3) There's _no pollution_.
4) But they do _spoil the view_. You need about _5000 wind turbines_ to replace _one coal-fired power station_ and 5000 of them cover _a lot_ of ground — that wouldn't look very nice at all.
5) There's also the problem of _no power when the wind stops_, and it's _impossible_ to _increase supply_ when there's _extra demand_.
6) The _initial costs are quite high_, but there are _no fuel costs_ and _minimal running costs_.

Hydroelectricity and Pumped Storage Systems

1) _Hydroelectric power_ usually requires the _flooding_ of a _valley_ by building a _big dam_.
2) _Rainwater_ is caught and allowed out _through turbines_. There is _no pollution_.
3) There is quite a _big impact_ on the _environment_ due to the flooding of the valley and possible _loss of habitat_ for some species. The reservoirs can also look very _unsightly_ when they _dry up_. Location in _remote valleys_ (in _Scotland_) tends to avoid these problems on the whole.

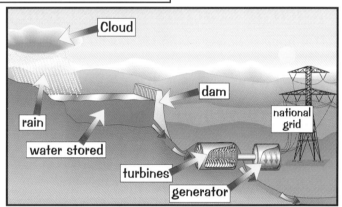

4) A _big advantage_ is _immediate response_ to increased demand and there's no problem with _reliability_ except in times of _drought_ — but remember this is _Scotland_ we're talking about!
5) _Initial costs are high_ but there's _no fuel_ and _minimal running costs_.

Pumped Storage Gives Extra Supply Just When it's Needed

1) Most large power stations have _huge boilers_ which have to be kept running _all night_ even though demand is _very low_. This means there's a _surplus_ of electricity at night.
2) It's surprisingly _difficult_ to find a way of _storing_ this spare energy for _later use_.
3) _Pumped storage_ is one of the _best solutions_ to the problem.
4) In pumped storage "spare" _night-time electricity_ is used to pump water up to a _higher reservoir_.
5) This can then be _released quickly_ during periods of _peak demand_ such as at _tea time_ each evening, to supplement the _steady delivery_ from the big power stations.
6) Remember, _pumped storage_ uses the same _idea_ as Hydroelectric Power but it _isn't_ a way of _generating_ power — but simply a way of _storing energy_ which has _already_ been generated.

Learn about Wind Power — it can blow your mind...

Lots of important details here on these nice green squeaky clean sources of energy — pity they make such a mess of the landscape. Three nice green squeaky clean _mini-essays_ please.

Wave Power and Tidal Power

Don't confuse _wave power_ with _tidal power_. They are _completely different_.

Wave Power — Lots of little Wave Converters

1) You need lots of small _wave generators_ located _around the coast_.
2) As waves come in to the shore they provide an _up and down motion_ which can be used to drive a _generator_.
3) There is _no pollution_. The main problems are _spoiling the view_ and being a _hazard to boats_.
4) They are _fairly unreliable_, since waves tend to die out when the _wind drops_.
5) _Initial costs are high_ but there's _no fuel_ and _minimal running costs_. Wave power is never likely to provide energy on a _large scale_ but it can be _very useful_ on _small islands_.

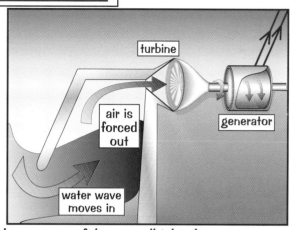

Tidal Barrages — Using The Sun and Moon's Gravity

1) _Tidal barrages_ are _big dams_ built across _river estuaries_ with _turbines_ in them.
2) As the _tide comes in_ it fills up the estuary to a height of _several metres_. This water can then be allowed out _through turbines_ at a controlled speed. It also drives the turbines on the way in.
3) There is _no pollution_. The source of the energy is the gravity of the Sun and the Moon.
4) The main problems are _preventing free access by boats_, _spoiling the view_ and possibly _altering habitats_ although this is _not certain_ since the tide comes _in and out anyway_.
5) Tides are _pretty reliable_ in the sense that they happen _twice a day without fail_, and always to the _predicted height_. The only drawback is that the _height_ of the tide is _variable_ so lower (neap) tides will provide _significantly less energy_ than the bigger "_spring_" tides. But tidal barrages are _excellent_ for _storing energy_ ready for periods of _peak demand_.
6) _Initial costs are moderately high_ but there's _no fuel_ and _minimal running costs_. Even though it can only be used in a _few_ of the _most suitable estuaries_ tidal power has the potential for generating a _significant amount_ of energy.

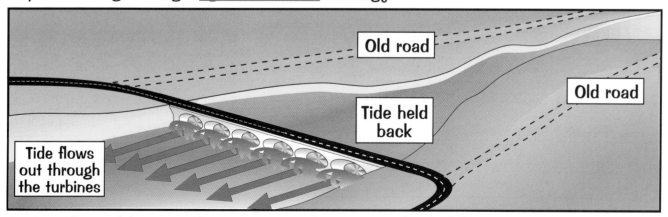

Don't confuse _tidal power_ with _wave power_. They are _completely different_.

Learn about Wave Power — and bid your cares goodbye...

I do hope you appreciate the big big differences between tidal power and wave power. They both involve salty sea water, sure — but there the similarities end. Lots of jolly details then, just waiting to be absorbed into your cavernous intra-cranial void. Smile and enjoy. And _learn_.

Geothermal and Wood Burning

Geothermal Energy — Heat From Underground

1) This is _only possible_ in _certain places_ where _hot rocks_ lie quite near to the _surface_. The source of much of the heat is the _slow decay_ of various _radioactive elements_ including _uranium_ deep inside the Earth.
2) _Water is pumped_ in pipes down to _hot rocks_ and _returns as steam_ to drive a _generator_.
3) This is actually _brilliant free energy_ with no real environmental problems.
4) The _main drawback_ is the _cost of drilling_ down _several km_ to the hot rocks.
5) Unfortunately there are _very few places_ where this seems to be an _economic option_ (for now).

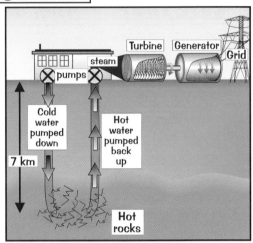

Wood Burning — Environmentally OK

1) This can be done _commercially_ on a _large scale_.
2) It involves the cultivation of _fast-growing trees_ which are then _harvested_, _chopped up_ and _burnt_ in a power station _furnace_ to produce _electricity_.
3) Unlike _fossil fuels_, wood burning does _not_ cause a problem with the _Greenhouse Effect_ because any CO_2 released in the burning of the wood was _removed_ when they _grew in the first place_, and because the trees are grown _as quickly as they are burnt_ they will _never run out_. This does _not apply_ to the burning of _rainforests_ where the trees take _much longer_ to grow.

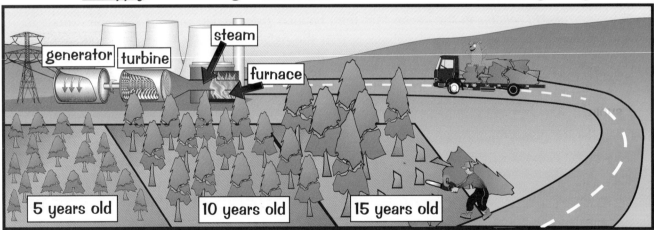

4) The _main drawback_ is the _use of land_ for _growing trees_, but if these woods can be made into _recreational areas_ then that may be a _positive benefit_ and certainly the woodlands should look quite _attractive_, as opposed to 5000 wind turbines covering miles and miles of countryside.
5) As a method of electricity generation wood burning may seem mighty _old-fashioned_, but if enough trees are grown this is a _reliable and plentiful source of energy_, with fewer environmental drawbacks than many other energy resources.
6) Initial costs _aren't too high_, but there's some cost in _harvesting and processing_ the wood.

Wood Burning to solve the energy crisis? — barking mad...

I must say I reckon on geothermal energy as being the big source of power for the next millennium or two. All you have to do is drill down 10 or 20km and you're sorted — limitless free energy. Anyway, two more squeaky clean _mini-essays_ just crying out to be _scribbled_. Enjoy.

SECTION FIVE — ENERGY

Solar Energy

LEARN the THREE different ways that solar energy can be harnessed:

1) Solar Cells Turn Sunlight Directly into Electric Current

1) _SOLAR CELLS_ generate _electric currents directly_ from sunlight.

2) They are quite _expensive initially_, but are a great way of providing a small amount of electricity _just about anywhere_.

3) Solar powered _calculators_ use them.

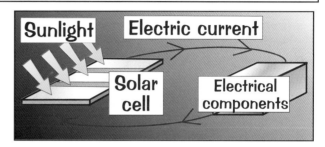

2) Solar Panels Simply Absorb Sunlight To Heat Water

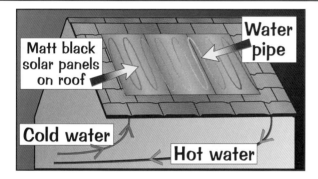

1) _SOLAR PANELS_ are much simpler than solar cells.

2) Solar panels simply contain _water pipes_ under a _black surface_.

3) _Heat radiation_ from the Sun is _absorbed_ by the _black surface_ to _heat the water_ in the pipes. It's as simple as that.

3) Solar Furnaces Produce Very High Temperatures

1) A _SOLAR FURNACE_ is a large array of _curved mirrors_ as shown in the picture.

2) These mirrors _focus_ a huge amount of sunlight onto _one spot_.

3) This produces _very high temperatures_ which are used to turn water into _steam_.

4) This _steam_ is then used to drive a _turbine_ which turns a _generator_ — just as in a normal power station, as shown on P. 75.

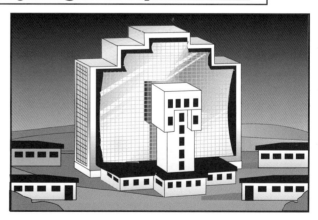

Solar Energy is Very Clean and Cheap

1) In all three cases there is _no pollution_.
2) In sunny countries solar power is a _very reliable source_ of energy — but only in the _daytime_.
3) Solar power will still provide _some energy_ even in _cloudy countries_ like Britain.
4) _Initial costs_ can be _high_ but after that the energy is _free_ and _running costs almost nil_ (apart from the _solar furnaces_ which are more complicated).

Solar Cells are like Fried Eggs — always best sunny side up...

Watch out for it — there are _three_ different ways of using solar power directly. _Learn_ all the details for all three, because they could ask you about any one of them. Solar energy is a very _typical_ renewable energy resource — _nice and clean_ but very dependent on the _weather_.

Revision Summary for Section Five

There are three distinct parts to Section Five. First there's power, work done, efficiency, etc. which involves a lot of formulae and calculations. Then there's heat transfer, which is trickier to fully get the grip of than most people realise, and finally there's the stuff on generating power, which is basically easy but there are lots of drivelly details to learn. Make sure you realise the different approach needed for all three bits and focus your planet-sized brain accordingly.

1) List the ten different types of energy, and give twelve different examples of energy transfers.
2) What's the connection between "work done" and "energy transferred"?
3) What's the formula for work done? A crazy dog drags a big branch 12m over the next-door neighbour's front lawn, pulling with a force of 535N. How much energy was transferred?
4) What's the formula for power? What are the units of power?
5) An electric motor uses 540kJ of electrical energy in 4½ minutes. What is its power consumption? If it has an efficiency of 85%, what's its power output?
6) Write down the Principle of the Conservation of Energy. When is energy actually *useful*?
7) Sketch the basic energy flow diagram for a typical "useful device".
8) What forms does the wasted energy always take?
9) What's the formula for efficiency? What are the three numerical forms suitable for efficiency?
10) Is efficiency really easy or really complicated? Find the efficiency for these machines:
   a) A motor which does 500J of useful work and in the process uses 800J of electricity.
   b) A steam train gets 2450kJ from the fuel and produces 412kJ of useful energy from it.
   c) A man eats 4512kJ of food energy and provides 320kJ of useful digging energy.
11) What causes heat to flow from one place to another? What do molecules do as they heat up?
12) Explain briefly the difference between conduction, convection and radiation.
13) Give a strict definition of conduction of heat and say which materials are good conductors.
14) Give a strict definition of convection. Give two examples of natural and forced convection.
15) List five properties of heat radiation. Which kind of objects emit and absorb heat radiation?
16) Which surfaces absorb heat radiation best? Which surfaces emit it best?
17) Describe two experiments to demonstrate the effect of different surfaces on radiant heat.
18) Describe insulation measures which reduce   a) conduction   b) convection   c) radiation.
19) Draw a fully labelled diagram of a Thermos Flask, and explain exactly what each bit is for.
20) List the seven main ways of insulating houses and say which are the most *effective* and which are the most *cost-effective* measures. How do you decide on cost-effectiveness?
21) Draw five energy chains which start with the Sun as the source of energy.
22) Nine out of the twelve energy resources originate in the Sun — which are they?
23) Which three energy resources do *not* originate in the Sun?
24) What exactly does it mean when a question says "Discuss..."?
25) List the eight kinds of renewable energy.
26) List the four non-renewable sources of energy and say why they are non-renewable.
27) List the advantages and disadvantages of using   a) renewables   b) non-renewables.
28) Which kind of resources do we get most of our energy from? Sketch a typical power station.
29) List seven environmental hazards with non-renewables and four ways that we can use less.
30) Give full details of how we can use wind power, including the advantages and disadvantages.
31) Give full details of how a hydroelectric scheme works. What's pumped storage all about?
32) Sketch a wave generator and explain the pros and cons of this as a source of energy.
33) Explain how tidal power can be harnessed. What are the pros and cons of this idea?
34) Explain where geothermal energy comes from. Describe how we can make use of it.
35) Explain the principles of wood-burning for generating electricity. Give the pros and cons.
36) Give brief details, with diagrams, for the three types of solar power.

Atomic Structure and Isotopes

See the Chemistry Book for a few more details on this.

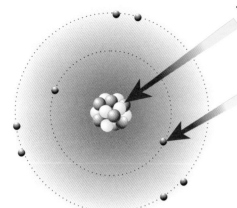

The *NUCLEUS* contains *protons* and *neutrons*.
Most of the *MASS* of the atom is contained in the *nucleus*,
but it takes up *virtually no space* — it's *tiny*.

The *ELECTRONS* fly around the *outside*.
They're *negatively charged* and really really *small*.
They *occupy a lot of space* and this gives the atom its
overall size, even though it's *mostly empty space*.

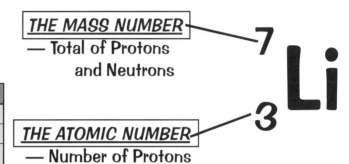

THE MASS NUMBER
— Total of Protons
and Neutrons

THE ATOMIC NUMBER
— Number of Protons

Make sure you *learn this table*:

PARTICLE	MASS	CHARGE
Proton	1	+1
Neutron	1	0
Electron	1/2000	-1

Isotopes are Different Forms of The Same Element

1) *Isotopes* are atoms with the *SAME number of protons* but a *DIFFERENT number of neutrons*.
2) Hence they have the *same atomic number*, but *different mass number*.
3) *Carbon-12 and Carbon-14* are good examples:
4) *Most elements* have different isotopes but there's usually only one or two *stable* ones.
5) The other isotopes tend to be *radioactive*, which means they *decay* into *other elements* and *give out radiation*. This is where all *radioactivity* comes from — *unstable radioactive isotopes* undergoing *nuclear decay* and spitting out *high energy particles*.

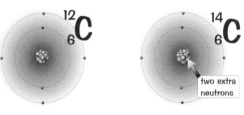

two extra neutrons

Rutherford's Scattering and The Demise of the Plum Pudding

1) In 1804 *John Dalton* said matter was made up of *tiny solid spheres* which he called *atoms*.
2) Later they discovered *electrons* could be *removed* from atoms. They then saw atoms as *spheres of positive charge* with tiny negative electrons *stuck in it* like plums in a *plum pudding*.
3) Then *Ernest Rutherford* and his merry men tried firing *alpha particles* at a *thin gold foil*. Most of them just went *straight through*, but the odd one came *straight back at them*, which was frankly a bit of a *shocker* for Ernie and his pals. Being pretty clued up guys though they realised this meant that *most of the mass* of the atom was concentrated *at the centre* in a *tiny nucleus*, with a *positive charge*. This means that most of an atom is just made up of *empty space*, which is *also a bit of a shocker* when you think about it.

Plum Pudding Theory — by 1911 they'd had their fill of it...

Yeah, that's right — atoms are mostly empty space. When you think about it, those electrons are amazing little jokers really. They have almost no mass, no size, and a tiny little -ve charge. In the end it's only their frantic whizzing about that makes atoms what they are. It's outrageous.

The Three Types of Radiation

Don't get _mixed up_ between _nuclear radiation_ which is _dangerous_ — and _electromagnetic radiation_ which _generally isn't_. Gamma radiation is included in both, of course.

Nuclear Radiation: Alpha, Beta and Gamma (α, β and γ)

You need to remember _two things_ about _each type of radiation_:
1) What they _actually are_   2) How well they _penetrate_ through stuff.

Alpha Particles

1) They are relatively _big_ and _heavy_ and _slow moving_.
2) They therefore _don't penetrate_ into materials but are _stopped quickly_.
3) They are actually _helium nuclei_: i.e. two _protons_ and two _neutrons_.

Beta Particles

1) These are _in between alpha and gamma_. They _penetrate quite well_, but not that well.
2) They move _quite fast_ and they are _quite small_.
3) They are actually just _ordinary electrons_, except they're moving _very fast_.

Gamma Rays

1) They are the _opposite of alpha particles_ in a way.
2) They _penetrate a long way_ into materials without being stopped.
3) They are _high energy EM waves_ with a very short wavelength.

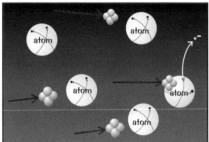
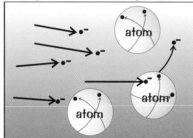
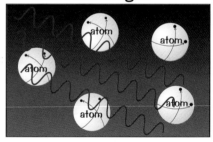

Remember What Blocks the Three Types of Radiation...

They like this for Exams, so _make sure you know_ what it takes to _block each of the three_:

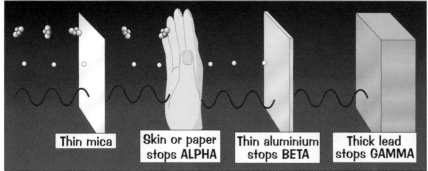

Thin mica | Skin or paper stops ALPHA | Thin aluminium stops BETA | Thick lead stops GAMMA

ALPHA particles blocked by _skin_ or _paper_.
BETA particles blocked by thin _aluminium_.
GAMMA rays blocked by _thick lead_.

Of course anything _equivalent_ will also block them, e.g. _spam_ will stop _alpha_, but _not_ the others; a thin sheet of _any metal_ will stop _beta_; and _very thick concrete_ will stop _gamma_ just like lead does.

Learn the three types of radiation — it's easy as abc...

Alpha, beta and gamma. You do realise those are just the first three letters of the Greek alphabet don't you: α, β, γ — just like a, b, c. They might sound like complex names to you but they were just easy labels at the time. Anyway, _learn all the facts_ about them — and _scribble_.

Detection Of Radiation

The Geiger-Müller Tube and Counter

1) This is the most _familiar type_ of _radiation detector_. You see them on TV documentaries going _click-click-clickety-click_, whilst the grim-faced reporter delivers his message of doom.

2) This is also the type used for _experiments in the lab_, as the counter allows you to record the number of _counts per minute_.

3) When an _alpha_, _beta_ or _gamma_ enters the _G-M tube_, it _ionises_ the gas inside and triggers an _electrical discharge_ (a spark) which makes a _clicking sound_ and also sends a _small signal_ to the electronic _counter_. It's so simple even I could have thought of it... but born too late. Sigh.

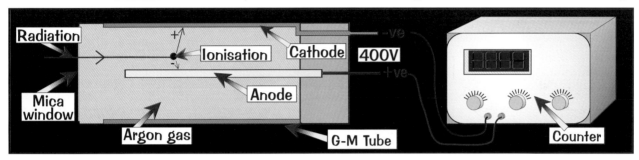

The _unit_ used for measuring _radioactivity_ is the _Becquerel_ (Bq). _One Becquerel_ is _one nucleus decaying per second_. So a count rate of _60 counts per minute (60 CPM)_ would represent _1 Bq_.

Photographic Film Also Detects Radiation

1) _Photographic film_ is another useful way of detecting radiation.

2) Workers in the _nuclear industry_ or those using _X-ray equipment_ such as _dentists_ and _radiographers_ wear _little blue badges_ which have a bit of _photographic film_ in them.

3) The film is checked _every now and then_ to see if it's got fogged _too quickly_, which would mean the person was getting _too much exposure_ to radiation.

The Radioactivity of a Sample Always Decreases Over Time

1) This is _pretty obvious_ when you think about it. Each time a _decay_ happens and an alpha, beta or gamma is given out, it means one more _radioactive nucleus_ has _disappeared_.

2) Obviously, as the _unstable nuclei_ all steadily disappear, the _activity as a whole_ will also _decrease_. So the _older_ a sample becomes, the _less radiation_ it will give out.

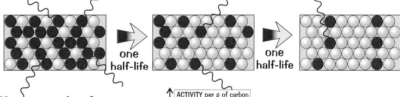

3) _How quickly_ the activity _drops off_ varies a lot from one radio-isotope to another. For _some_ it can take _just a few hours_ before nearly all the unstable nuclei have _decayed_, whilst others can last for _millions of years_.

4) The term _HALF-LIFE_ is used to indicate _how long_ the radioactivity of a sample _lasts_. The _longer_ the half-life, the _longer_ the sample will remain radioactive. Simple.

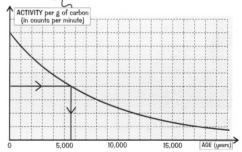

Definition of Half-life — a freshly woken teenager...

Make sure you remember those two ways of measuring radiation: G-M tube and photographic film, and remember what a Becquerel is. This page is ideal for the good old mini-essay method I reckon, just to make sure you've taken all the important points on board. _Learn and scribble_.

Background Radiation

Radioactivity is a Totally Random Process

Unstable nuclei will _decay_ and in the process _give out radiation_. This process is entirely _random_. This means that if you have 1000 unstable nuclei, you can't say when _any one of them_ is going to decay, and neither can you do anything at all _to make a decay happen_.
Each nucleus will just decay quite _spontaneously_ in its _own good time_. It's completely unaffected by _physical_ conditions like _temperature_ or by any sort of _chemical bonding_ etc.

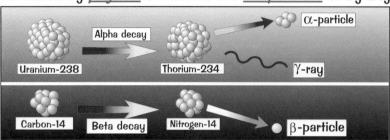

When the nucleus _does_ decay it will _spit out_ one or more of the three types of radiation, _alpha_, _beta_ or _gamma_, and in the process the _nucleus_ will often _change_ into a _new element_.

Background Radiation Comes From Many Sources

Natural background radiation comes from:

1) Radioactivity of naturally occurring _unstable isotopes_ which are _all around us_ — in the _air_, in _food_, in _building materials_ and in the _rocks_ under our feet.

2) Radiation from _space_, which is known as _cosmic rays_. These come mostly from the _Sun_.

3) Radiation due to _human activity_, i.e. _fallout_ from _nuclear explosions_ or _dumped nuclear waste_. But this represents a _tiny_ proportion of the total background radiation.

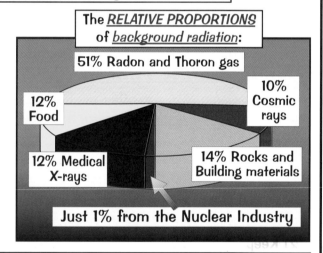

The _RELATIVE PROPORTIONS_ of _background radiation_:

51% Radon and Thoron gas
10% Cosmic rays
12% Food
12% Medical X-rays
14% Rocks and Building materials
Just 1% from the Nuclear Industry

The Level of Background Radiation Changes, Depending on Where You Are

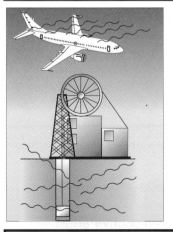

Millom

Coloured bits indicate more radiation from rocks

1) At _high altitudes_ (e.g. in _jet planes_) it _increases_ because of more exposure to _cosmic rays_.

2) _Underground in mines_, etc. it increases because of the _rocks_ all around.

3) Certain _underground rocks_ can cause higher levels at the _surface_, especially if they release _radioactive radon gas_, which tends to get _trapped inside people's houses_. This varies widely across the UK depending on the _rock type_, as shown:

Background Radiation — it's no good burying your head in the sand...

Yip, it's funny old stuff is radiation, that's for sure. It is quite mysterious, I guess, but just like anything else, the _more you learn about it_, the _less_ of a mystery it becomes. This page is positively bristling with simple straightforward facts about radiation. Three tiny little _mini-essays_ practised two or three times and all this knowledge will be yours — forever. Enjoy. ☺

Radiation Hazards and Safety

Radiation Harms Living Cells

1) *Alpha*, *beta* and *gamma* radiation will cheerfully *enter living cells* and *collide with molecules*.
2) These collisions cause *ionisation*, which *damages or destroys* the *molecules*.
3) *Lower doses* tend to cause *minor damage* without *killing* the cell.
4) This can produce *mutant cells* which *divide uncontrollably*. This is *cancer*.
5) *Higher doses* tend to *kill cells completely*, which causes *radiation sickness* if a lot of your body cells *all get blatted at once*.
6) The *extent* of the harmful effects depends mainly on *how long you're exposed* to the radiation, and also *how strong* the source of radiation is.

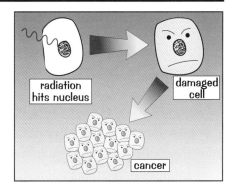
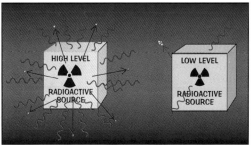

You Need to Learn About These Safety Precautions

1) If you don't *already know* that radioactive materials need to be handled *carefully* then you must be some sort of *idiot*.
2) In the Exam they might ask you to *list some specific precautions* that should be taken when *handling radioactive materials*.
3) If you want those *easy marks* you'd better learn all these:

In the School Laboratory:

1) *Never* allow *skin contact* with a source. Always handle with *tongs*.
2) Keep the source at *arm's length* to keep it *as far* from the body *as possible*.
3) Keep the source *pointing away* from the body and *avoid looking directly at it*.
4) *Always* keep the source in a *lead box* and put it back in *as soon* as the experiment is *over*.

Extra Precautions for Industrial Nuclear Workers:

1) Wearing of *full protective suits* to prevent *tiny radioactive particles* from being *inhaled* or lodging *on the skin* or *under fingernails* etc.
2) Use of *lead-lined suits* and *lead/concrete barriers* and *thick lead windows* to prevent exposure to *γ-rays* from highly contaminated areas. (α and β are stopped *much more easily*.)
3) Use of *remotely controlled robot arms* in highly radioactive areas.

Radiation Sickness — well yes, it does all get a bit tedious...

Quite a few picky details here. It's easy to kid yourself that you don't really need to know all this stuff. Well take it from me, you *do* need to know it all and there's only one surefire way to find out whether you do or not. Three *mini-essays* please, with all the picky details in. Enjoy.

Uses of Radioactive Materials

This is a *nice easy bit* of *straightforward learning*. Below are the *seven main uses* for radioactive isotopes. Make sure you *learn all the details*.
In particular, make sure you get the grip of why each application uses a *particular radio-isotope* according to its *half-life* and the *type of radiation* it gives out.

1) Tracers in Medicine — always Short Half-life γ-emitters

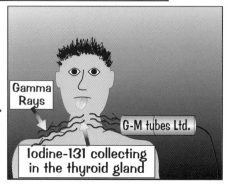

Gamma Rays

G-M tubes Ltd.

Iodine-131 collecting in the thyroid gland

1) Certain *radioactive isotopes* can be *injected* into people (or they can just *swallow* them) and their progress *around the body* can be followed using a *detector* (such as a G-M tube) which will show where the *strongest reading* is coming from.
2) A good example is radioactive *Iodine-131* which is used to check that the *thyroid gland* in the throat is working properly.
3) *All isotopes* which are taken *into the body* must *always* be GAMMA sources (never alpha or beta), so that the radiation *passes out of the body* and they should only last *a few hours*, so that the radioactivity inside the patient *quickly disappears*. (i.e. they should have a *short half-life*.)

2) Tracers in Industry — For Finding Leaks

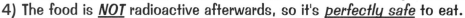

G-M tubes Ltd.

1) Radio-isotopes can be used to *detect leaks in pipes*.
2) You just *squirt it in*, and then go along the *outside* of the pipe with a *detector* to find places of *extra high* radioactivity, which shows the stuff is *leaking out*. This is really useful for *concealed* or *underground* pipes, to save you *digging up half the road* trying to find the leak.
3) The isotope used *must* be a *gamma emitter*, so that the radiation can be *detected* even through *metal or earth* which may be *surrounding* the pipe. Alpha and beta rays wouldn't be much use because they are *easily blocked* by any surrounding material.
4) It should also have a *short half-life* so as not to cause a *hazard* if it collects somewhere.

3) Sterilisation of Food and Surgical Instruments Using γ-Rays

unsterilised

Gamma source

sterilised

1) *Food* can be exposed to a *high dose* of *gamma rays* which will *kill* all *microbes* thus keeping the food *fresh for longer*.
2) *Medical instruments* can be *sterilised* in just the same way, rather than *boiling them*.
3) The great *advantage* of *irradiation* over boiling is that it doesn't involve *high temperatures* so things like *fresh apples* or *plastic instruments* can be totally *sterilised* without *damaging* them.
4) The food is *NOT* radioactive afterwards, so it's *perfectly safe* to eat.

4) Radiotherapy — the Treatment of Cancer Using γ-Rays

1) Since high doses of gamma rays will *kill all living cells* they can be used to *treat cancers*.
2) The gamma rays have to be *directed carefully* and at just the right *dosage* so as to kill the *cancer cells* without damaging too many *normal cells*.
3) However, a *fair bit of damage* is *inevitably* done to *normal cells* which makes the patient feel *very ill*. But if the cancer is *successfully killed off* in the end, then it's worth it.

Uses of Radioactive Materials

5) Thickness Control in Industry and Manufacturing

This is a classic application and is _pretty popular in Exams_. It's pretty simple really.

1) You have a _radioactive source_ and you direct it _through the stuff being made_, usually a continuous sheet of _paper_ or _cardboard_ or _metal_ etc.

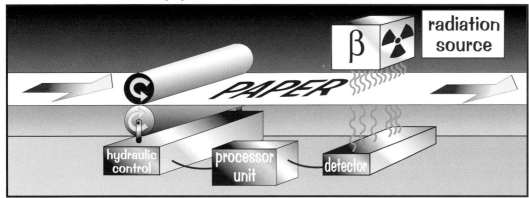

2) The _detector_ is on the _other side_ and is connected to a _control unit_.

3) When the amount of radiation detected _goes down_, it means the stuff is coming out _too thick_ and so the control unit _pinches the rollers up_ a bit to make it _thinner_ again.

4) If the reading _goes up_, it means it's _too thin_, so the control unit _opens the rollers out_ a bit.
   It's all clever stuff, but the most _important thing_, as usual, is the _choice of isotope_.

5) First of all it must have a _nice long half-life_ (of several _years_ at least!), otherwise the strength would _gradually decline_ and the silly control unit would keep _pinching up the rollers_ trying to _compensate_.

6) Secondly, the source must be a _BETA source_ for _paper and cardboard_, or a _GAMMA source_ for _metal sheets_. This is because the stuff being made must _PARTLY_ block the radiation. If it _all_ goes through (or _none_ of it does), then the reading _won't change_ at all as the thickness changes. Alpha particles are no use for this since they would _all be stopped_.

6) Radioactive Dating of Rocks and Archaeological Specimens

1) The discovery of radioactivity and the idea of _half-life_ gave scientists their _first chance_ to _accurately_ work out the _age_ of _rocks_ and _fossils_ and _archaeological specimens_.

2) By measuring the _amount_ of a _radioactive isotope_ left in a sample, and knowing its _half-life_, you can work out _how long_ the thing has been around.

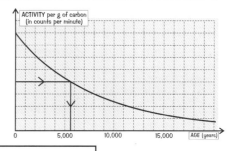

7) Generating Power from Nuclear Fuel (Uranium)

1) _Radioactive decay_ always _gives out energy_ in the form of _heat_.

2) The radioactive decay _inside the Earth_ is responsible for much of the _heat_ down there.

3) By _purifying uranium_, we can set up a _chain reaction_ where each decay causes another one. In this way we can _increase the rate of reaction_ to generate _lots of heat_ and then use it to produce _electricity_. This is what a nuclear power station does (see P. 75).

Will any of that be in your Exam? — isotope so...

First _learn_ the seven headings till you can write them down _from memory_. Then start _learning_ all the details that go with each one of them. As usual, the best way to check what you know is to do a _mini-essay_ for each section. Then check back and see what details you _missed_. Nicely.

88

Revision Summary for Section Six

It's an outrage — just so much stuff you've gotta learn — it's all work, work, work, no time to rest, no time to play. But then that's the grim cruel reality of life in 1990s Britain — just drudgery, hard work and untold weariness...   "And then he woke up and it had all been a dream..." Yeah, maybe life's not so bad after all — even for hard-done-to teenagers. Just a few jolly bits and bobs to learn in warm, cosy, comfortable civilisation. Practise these questions over and over again till you can answer them all effortlessly.   Smile and enjoy.   ☺

1) Sketch an atom. Give three details about the nucleus and three details about the electrons.
2) Draw up a wee table detailing the mass and charge of the three basic subatomic particles.
3) Explain what the mass number and atomic number of an atom represent.
4) Explain what isotopes are.
5) What is the best known pair of isotopes?
6) Are most isotopes stable or unstable? What happens to unstable isotopes?
7) What was the Plum Pudding Model of the atom? Who put paid to that crazy old idea?
8) Describe Rutherford's Scattering Experiment with a diagram and say what happened.
9) What was the inevitable conclusion to be drawn from this experiment.
10) What is the main difference between EM radiation and nuclear radiation?
11) Describe in detail what the three types of radiation, α, β, and γ, actually are.
12) How do the three types compare in terms of how well they penetrate into materials?
13) List several things which will block α-particles.
14) List several things which will block β-particles.
15) List several things which will block γ-rays.
16) What is a Geiger-Müller tube and counter used for?
17) Draw a labelled diagram of a Geiger-Müller tube and explain briefly how it works.
18) What units is radioactivity measured in? How many of those units is equal to 120cpm?
19) What are the two common methods of detecting radioactivity? Which is the simplest?
20) Sketch a diagram to show how the number of radioactive nuclei in a sample keeps halving.
21) What does the "half-life" of a sample tell us about it?
22) How long and how short can half-lives be?
23) Sketch a typical graph showing how the activity of a sample falls over a period of time.
24) "Radioactive decay is a totally random process". What does this mean?
25) Can we do anything to cause a nucleus to undergo radioactive decay?
26) Sketch a fairly accurate pie chart to show the six main sources of background radiation.
27) List three places where the level of background radiation is increased and explain why.
28) Exactly what kind of damage does radiation do inside body cells?
29) What damage do low doses cause?   What effects do higher doses have?
30) List four safety precautions for the school lab., and three more for nuclear workers.
31) Describe in detail how radioactive isotopes are used in each of the following:
   a) tracers in medicine   b) tracers in industry   c) sterilisation   d) thickness control
   e) treating cancer   f) dating of rock samples   g) generating power.

Answers

P.15 **1)** 339.2N **2)** 3Ω **3)** 106J **4)** 10N/cm²			
P.23 Revision Summary **25) a)** 0.125A **b)** 5000N/cm² **c)** 37.4kg **d)** 321W **e)** 240V **f)** 10A			
P.39 Revision Summary **17)** 0.09m/s **18)** 137m **21)** 35m/s² **22)** 4.4 m/s²			
P.49 1) 198m **2)** 490m			
P.53 Revision Summary **31)** 1980m **32)** 0.86s **33)** 74.3m			
P.60 Revision Summary **35)** 9½ million million km **36)** 228,000 yrs **37)** Real strange, The Bentley Turbo			
P.80 Revision Summary **3)** 6420J **5)** 2000W, 1700W **10) a)** 62.5% **b)** 16.8% **c)** 7.1%			
P.88 Revision Summary **18)** 2Bq			

SECTION SIX — RADIOACTIVITY

Index

Index

Index

Index